W9-AVW-000

BUSY, STRESSED, AND FOOD OBSESSED!

LISA LEWTAN

About The Author

Lisa Lewtan is a Healthy Living Strategist and the founder of Healthy, Happy, and Hip. Using the skills she developed as a successful technology entrepreneur, Lisa self-hacked her own mind and body to restore her health and then go on to feel better than ever.

A graduate of the Institute for Integrative Nutrition, Lisa now helps highly successful superwomen to slow down, chill out, develop a better relationship with food, look good, and feel great. She offers private coaching, workshops, online courses, and women's retreats.

Lisa's Eat to Thrive program was profiled in the Boston Globe and her articles have been featured in numerous publications including The Huffington Post, Better After 50, and MindBodyGreen.

www.HealthyHappyandHip.com

PRAISE FOR THE BOOK AND AUTHOR

PROFESSIONAL ENDORSEMENTS:

"Busy, Stressed and Food Obsessed is a rich and powerful book which provides a roadmap to understanding yourself and your body. Lewtan's book is one of the most important works you will ever read. She takes you through a thoughtful process to understand where you are today and she shares tried and true strategies to help you reach a new and improved you. What sets Lisa Lewtan apart is that she has been busy, stressed and food obsessed and understands it all and can provide meaningful ways to help you achieve a new level of transformation physically, emotionally, and spiritually. Her advice actually works and you will be amazed at how little lifestyle adjustments produce major changes in the way you feel. Lisa Lewtan is simply brilliant and a great life coach!" **- Christine Schuster, President & CEO, Emerson Hospital**

"Lisa Lewtan puts into words the real issues around food, health, and mood. Integrating her personal journey and real life happenings, she presents a simple, readable format that is a valuable tool for anyone who is eager to do the work to transform their life!" - **Marcy Balter, Board Chair, Kripalu Center for Yoga and Health**

"Lisa Lewtan's book is not just another diet. It is an easy to read guide for helping people find their own path to a healthy lifestyle."
- Rachel A. Haims, M.D. Instructor of Medicine, Harvard Medical School

"Lisa Lewtan doesn't pontificate from a health and nutrition perch of righteousness. She's been right there in the trenches with the millions of women like you and me who struggle daily with eating, weight, and

self-esteem issues. But watch out! Lisa is on a mission to get you good with these struggles and no one else does it quite like her. If you're "busy, stressed and food obsessed" -- and nothing you do seems to help change that -- read this book. If you're looking for a book that has you saying, "Yup, that's me," at least a hundred times...you've found it. Thank you, Lisa, for getting it -- and for your candor, and solid, kickass advice."
- Abby Rodman, best-selling author of Without This Ring

"Are you obsessed with food? This book reminds us to take the time to listen to what we tell ourselves about what, why and when we choose to eat. It urges us to listen to our body, create self-awareness and give ourselves permission to understand the habits, triggers, cravings and rituals that lead to unconscious eating. Take a break from the "busyness" and chaos of the day on autopilot and slow down, enjoy your life, practice self-care and develop a new relationship with food and self that truly nourishes the mind, emotions, spirit and body." **- Kathryn McKinnon, Time Management Expert & Speaker, Harvard Business School Executive Coach, Author of Best Seller on Amazon, Triple Your Time Today!**

"Lisa Lewtan has given us a smart, comprehensive and sane approach to food and the role it plays—for good or ill—in our stress level and our quality of life. That said, this book doesn't only offer solutions for the "food-obsessed." In a wonderfully down-to-earth, inviting, 'you-can-do-this' way, Lisa gives a recipe for healthy living to all women who suffer from the effects of life in a crazy-busy world. What a beautiful and much-needed invitation to seek and find what we are truly hungry for."
- Abby Seixas, author of Finding the Deep River Within; A Woman's Guide to Recovering Balance and Meaning in Everyday Life.

"A wonderful read, "Busy, Stressed and Food Obsessed" lets you know that the person most in charge of your happiness and success is yourself. Written with humor, honesty, brave energy and examples from her own clinical experience, Lisa Lewtan's easy approach to many of life's frequent problems asks you to honestly question yourself. By asking you to see how you think negatively about yourself, she shows, often by example, how this can deeply affect your life. Her guide helps to make food what it should be – a source of enjoyment and nourishment, instead of what is hurting us, both emotionally and physically." **- Ina Stephens, MD, RYT, FAAP - Associate Professor of Pediatrics and Medical Education - University of Virginia Medical Center**

"Lisa Lewtan possesses a unique understanding of modern American women. Her book offers a beautiful blend of personal experience and practical insight that can help women examine their relationship with food and activate workable plans. I am especially impressed with the connections she makes between mindfulness, wellness, and what we consume. Cheers to Lisa!" **- Jamie Marich, Ph.D., LPCC-S, LICDC-CS, Creator of the Dancing Mindfulness community and author of "Dancing Mindfulness," psychotherapist and educator on trauma and addiction issues**

"Lisa invites us to quit judging ourselves. She plays the role of a kind friend gently reminding us to chill out and simply observe what is making us stressed and food obsessed. In this book, Lisa helps us discover our triggers and gives us the right tools for self-compassion and success." **- Tania Green, CEO and Founder of PMS Bites**

"Lisa Lewtan is the picture of positivity, ingenuity and healthy productivity. Read her book "Busy, Stressed, & Food Obsessed!" and uncover the secrets to her success!" **- Dr. Kathleen M. LeMaitre, MD, FACOG Medical Staff President St. Elizabeth's Medical Center**

CLIENT ENDORSEMENTS:

"Lisa taught me that in order to succeed I needed to stop fighting with food and embrace what is good for me both mentally and physically. I am proud to say that food is no longer my enemy and that I am not the least bit attracted to putting anything into my body that does not benefit my overall health and wellbeing." **- Marci Cohen**

"If you are at a point where you're sick of hearing your own excuses but don't want a drill sergeant food cop breathing down your neck either, call Lisa. She's JUST what the doctor ordered. Literally. **-Lena West**

"Meeting with Lisa one-on-one was HUGE for me. A mind shift of looking at all this as a privilege and a choice—not a punishment or a soul crushing diet full of self-loathing!" **- Tara Gold**

"I met with Lisa and she exuded health, positivity and joy. There was no fluff. We both knew what help I needed. I realized that it wasn't just about sugar, it was about life. Lisa is not just a health coach. Lisa is a life coach helping us design healthy ways to attain what we want. I'm forever grateful." **- Claudia Crain**

"Lisa has given me the confidence to realize that I matter as much as those I care for and that I can have the things I want for myself because I deserve them. She showed me that the power to change was inside me all along and, for that, I will always be grateful." **- Rose Hattabaugh**

"I have totally changed my eating habits to a much healthier diet. Stress eating was part of my life, and now I have healthy choices when I have to eat on the go. I recommend Lisa's gentle way of changing your habits to healthy choices that will make you so much happier in the long run." **- Carolyn Ross**

"The last five pounds are always the hardest. Lisa helped me to tweak my lifestyle to help lose the weight slowly while learning how to maintain my goal for a lifetime." **- Laura Efron**

"While I consider myself a healthy person, Lisa gave me strategies to be able to live a healthy lifestyle with food and wellbeing no matter what situation life throws my way and I am forever thankful."
- Samantha Bartfield

"Working with Lisa, I realized that I had been feeding my anxiety with food, and once I began feeding myself with the things I really needed, I recognized my poor food habits for what they were. Lisa's gift is in teaching her clients how to care for themselves. If your mind and soul are being nourished, the body will follow." **- Carol Spann**

"Beyond the food/body connection, Lisa helped me with my soul. She gave me tools to make conscious decisions about my inner soul health. Thank you, thank you Lisa, for being a genuine friend and mentor."
- Olivia Wakefield

"With a degree in nutrition, I knew that healthy balance was important. However, in my late fifties, all I wanted was sugar! My doctor saw the ten pound weight gain in a year and told me to lose it! Then, I met Lisa! I'm back to feeling like I always have. I'm happy, I feel great and eat anything I want in moderation. Meeting Lisa and listening to my body is the BEST thing I have done for myself. I deserve to feel good."
- Mindy Shanfeld

"When you work with Lisa Lewtan, prepare to see yourself in a new light. I have participated in the Eat to Thrive workshop as well as in one-on-one coaching with Lisa. In each instance, Lisa's ability to see through the issue is liberating. Liberating because the issue is now in front of you, and you have the clarity to either do nothing or work through the situation. Lisa is kind and supportive. She pushes you just hard enough to propel yourself forward." **- Mark Curelop**

"I just want to thank Lisa for helping me go through a self-discovery process that brought me to where I am today. I think she is the best. She is a therapist, educator, friend, and I just adore her. From day one, there was a connection that you don't always find. She not only helped me with nutrition issues, but she was my life coach. I have grown and changed in so many ways. Thank you, Lisa!!!" **- Lauren Corkin**

BUSY, STRESSED, AND FOOD OBSESSED!

Calm Down, Ditch Your Inner-Critic Bitch, and
Finally Figure out What Your Unique Body Needs to Thrive

The content of this book is for general instruction only. Each person's physical, mental, emotional, and spiritual condition is unique. The instruction in this book is not intended to replace or interrupt the reader's relationship with a physician or other professional. Please consult your doctor for matters pertaining to your specific health and diet.

Because of the dynamic nature of the internet, any web addresses or links contained in this book may have changed since publication and may no longer be valid.

The views expressed in this work are solely those of the author and do not necessarily reflect the views of the publisher, and the publisher hereby disclaims any responsibility for them.

Every effort has been made to protect the privacy of individuals in the writing of this book. All the client stories included in the book are composites aggregated over years of experience. The character names for clients are fictional and invented. Any resemblance to actual persons, living or dead, or actual events is purely coincidental.

If expert assistance or counseling is needed, the services of a trained professional should be sought. Any application of the material in the following pages is at the reader's discretion and their sole responsibility.

To stay in contact with the author, visit www.healthyhappyandhip.com

ISBN-10: 0692500510
ISBN-13: 978-0-692-50051-4
Printed in the United States of America

Library of Congress Control Number: 2015918228
Healthy, Happy & Hip: Waltham, Massachusetts

In memory of
Harold, Hero, and Marvin who, respectively, taught me how to
Live, Love, and Laugh.

"*To read without reflecting is like eating without digesting.*"

-Edmund Burke

FOREWORD
by: Marilena Minucci

One of the first and most intimate relationships a woman develops is with food. If there were a social media status assigned to this connection, there would be only one obvious choice: IT'S COMPLICATED.

But how did it get this way?

It's clear that the role of food and the messages we hear about eating in our early years have a direct impact on our sense of self, our wellbeing, and our ability to thrive, relax, and enjoy life.

Food is quickly given "other duties as assigned," and we go from fueling our bodies to "using" food as a "drug of choice" for so many other purposes than for which it was intended.

In the midst of all this, we have the contradictory illusion that our insanity with food is the only thing that keeps us sane. We think it serves us when, in fact, exactly the opposite is true. It runs like malware in the background of our operating systems, slowing down our ability to function or perform to our full potential.

Think about it. What percentage of your energy and time is taken up with food thoughts, suppressing your hunger, or talking yourself out of a craving? Now, think about what would be available to you if all that were to just go away? What space would open up within you?

It's conflicting and confusing at best. It keeps us stuck because the most important question is not really being asked: Why? Why do YOU think about and use food the way you do?

We deserve to uncover the reasons why we get in our own way. At the very least, this is the first step to finding our freedom from food obsession and creating the health and life we desire.

It is only when we feel supported on many levels that things can begin to shift and we can consider letting go of what truly does not serve us.

So what are you tolerating that compels you to hold on to your stress and anything less than a healthy and delicious relationship with food? Aren't you exhausted? When will enough be enough?

It is no accident that you have come to this place and opened this book. Clearly, you are looking for another way. It is possible to live differently. This is not another diet full of deprivation but an invitation to unwrap many gifts that are waiting to be revealed to you.

I have a feeling that this book has the potential to change your life. These are tricky waters to navigate alone. What will change if you put down this book now? What will be different in six days, six months, or six years?

If what we think about expands, then we need to shift our thoughts away from food and overwhelm and focus on loving and nourishing ourselves in a healthier way. This is precisely the gift Lisa Lewtan is offering you here.

She is willing to go where women don't often like to go. She is in the bottom of your purse or the back of the desk drawer. She is in the can of frosting you keep hidden in the freezer or hanging out with your secret stash.

Lisa creates a safe space inspired by her own experiences so you can embark on a journey where it is okay to be hungry and actually use that hunger as a compass to reconnect with yourself.

The irreverent deep-down-to-your-soul-truths told in these pages may make you laugh and sometimes cry, but most of all, will offer a witness to tell you:

-You are not crazy...
-You can find peace within yourself...
-It is possible to be at home within your body....
And it need not be COMPLICATED at all.

Enjoy this journey.

Marilena Minucci, MS, CHC, BCC
www.QuantumCoachingMethod.com

TABLE OF CONTENTS

TABLE OF CONTENTS

I BELIEVE...

I believe that you are not crazy, even if you think about food all day.

I believe that willpower is for superheroes.

I believe that you will feel much better if you slow down and breathe deeply.

I believe that people will remember you for how you made them feel, not for how much you weighed.

I believe that you will not benefit from beating yourself up.

I believe that you should move your body to feel alive, not to punish yourself.

I believe that hunger is our body telling us it needs something.

I believe that you are not broken and, therefore, do not need to be fixed.

I believe that diets don't work, but strategies do.

I believe that you will not feel better for eating that cookie.

I believe that food should not be labeled good or bad, but rather "more often" or "less often."

I believe that you are not lazy, just tired.

I believe that when it comes to eating, we should get rid of words like "cheat," "bad," and "deserve."

I believe that your body talks to you but if you don't quiet your mind, you can't hear it.

I believe that happiness is a choice.

I believe that we must take responsibility for our own health.

I believe that gratitude and purpose are keys to a fulfilling life.

I believe that self-compassion is essential for good health.

I believe that it's not about how many times you get off track, it's about how many times you get back on.

I believe that it's not about being perfect, it's about being consistent most of the time.

I believe in YOU.

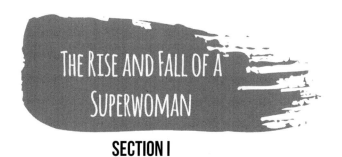

The Rise and Fall of a Superwoman

SECTION I

CHAPTER 1

I Get It. I Lived It. But Not Anymore.

"My mission in life is not merely to survive, but to thrive; and to do so with some passion, some compassion, some humor, and some style."

- Maya Angelou

For those of us who are busy, stressed, and food obsessed, sometimes food is our best friend and, at other times, our worst enemy. We eat because we are tired, happy, sad, lonely, anxious, bored, excited, triggered, and sometimes, when we are actually hungry.

We eat in the car, while on the phone, while watching TV or on the computer, while reading books, while making dinner, and hopefully, sometimes, even while sitting at a table.

Some of us eat healthy one day and not the next. Some of us feel good about our bodies and what they look like on the outside (at least on some days), and some of us absolutely do not ever feel good about the way we look.

Some of us, despite that fact that we look like we have perfect bodies, are agonizing over the last five pounds, and some of us, despite the fact that we are fit and happy, are tormented because we are seen as overweight.

Some of us are very controlling about what we eat, and some of us are very controlled by what we eat.

Some of us count calories all day long, survive on fake food, or try to eat how we deem to be absolutely perfectly, sometimes to a fault.

For all of us, food is an issue. An issue that can, at times, make us feel crazy.

I Get It. I Lived It. But Not Anymore.

After twenty years of trial and error, I have slowly discovered my own unique "Healthy, Happy, and Hip" lifestyle plan so that I can finally relax about food, stop beating myself up, and have more mental energy to enjoy my life.

My goal with this book is to teach you how to follow your own clues and design your own lifestyle plan. I will set you up with key strategies that will help you end your food frustrations and allow you to focus on enjoying YOUR life.

In this book, I will teach you how to calm down, eat healthier, stop beating yourself up, stop obsessing about food, and put an end to the soul-crushing, self-loathing feelings that often accompany deprivation diets.

I will walk with you through the exact system I used to connect my own dots and that helped me transform my life. I will give you all the tips, tools, and tricks I use to help my clients. I will hold your hand every step of the way and will guide you as your new best friend, your food therapist, and the personal cheerleader you always needed but never found.

But....If you are looking for a tough love health bully, then shut this book right now.

I refuse to beat you up.
I refuse to make you feel like a piece of shit.
I refuse to encourage your super perfectionist tendencies.

Why?
Because I know you are already doing that to yourself.
And it doesn't work.
And right here, right now, I want you to stop.

As we embark on this investigative journey together, I am not going to get into the nitty gritty details about proteins, fats, carbs, and supplements. Nor am I going to talk about the pros and cons of eating paleo, raw, vegan, etc. There are hundreds of other people out there doing that already.

Instead, I make the case that if you are ready to slow down and take responsibility for really embracing the causes of your hunger and food obsession, and if you are really ready to challenge your own thought patterns and get to know your own body, YOUR BODY will teach you how to best take care of it.

YOU already have the power inside of you to get healthy and feel great. We just need to access that power.

Once you are ready to make your health a priority and to solve the mysteries of your particular, miraculous body, I can help you begin to connect all the dots. Everything, including your weight, will fall almost magically into place.

Why Should You Listen to Me?
Look, I am not a doctor and I am not a dietician. I am, however, uniquely qualified to help you with your busy, stressed, and food obsessed issues because:

I understand you.

I've done the bootstrapped, working 24/7, high-tech entrepreneur thing, and I've done the diehard volunteer thing, and I've done the full-time mom thing. I know how hard it can be to get dinner on the table and to find a healthy snack while on the road. I understand the social pressures of alcohol and eating out all the time, and I know how hard it is to relax when there is always so much to do.

I have done it all and have literally collapsed trying to keep it all together.

I am a reformed sugar addict and remain a reformed superwoman with a very big appetite who understands how the number on a scale can ruin your whole day. I love food. I love buying it, preparing it, eating it, reading about it, talking about it, taking pictures of it, and even complaining about it.

"I AM A WORK IN PROGRESS AND I KNOW I'M NOT PERFECT. BUT I'M OK WITH THAT."

-LISA LEWTAN

Unlike most of you, however, I've spent the last twenty years studying nutrition theories, meditation, the mind-body connection and fitness in order to self-hack and heal my own mind and body.

I am a graduate of the Institute for Integrative Nutrition and have a successful coaching practice where I help highly successful superwomen slow down, chill-out, develop a better relationship with food, look good, and feel great.

As a Healthy Living Strategist and the founder of Healthy, Happy, and Hip, I have also had the privilege of running workshops, retreats, and support groups for clients on a regular basis.

I talk to women about food all the time and I never get tired of hearing their stories, their frustrations, their insights, and their solutions.

I collect strategies and tips that I have spent years testing out and improving and now, with this book, I am ready to share them with you.

Most importantly though, the reason you want to listen to me is that I FEEL GREAT. In fact, I'm in my fifties and I feel better than EVER.

Even though I still think about food a lot and I still love food, food does not make me crazy anymore. (Well, at least most of the time! I mean, I am human!)

Food for Thought:
To get daily doses of inspiration, come join my Facebook community.

I've got an exercise routine of my own that is fun, varied, and a joy rather than a punishment.

My life works, my relationships work, my business works, AND my body works.

I walk my walk and talk my talk and have been putting in the time, doing the work, and reaping the benefits from this "Healthy, Happy and Hip" way I've found to totally transform my body, mind, and life.

But it wasn't always this way...

CHAPTER II

How THIS Cookie Crumbled

"Take care of your body. It's the only place you have to live."
-Jim Rohn

Growing up, I was a very picky eater unless it came to junk food. I liked pizza and I liked ice cream. I loved cupcakes. My daily lunch was a home packed sack with a tuna sandwich on white bread, a devil dog, and a can of Hawaiian Punch.

Although I was sick all the time and walked around with big dark circles under my eyes, I was smart in school and I was skinny, so nobody cared about what I ate. By the time I was a teenager, I was still eating mostly crap and, in my mind, was thought of as a smart, skinny girl, which felt terribly uninteresting to me.

I wasn't an athlete, a musician, or a dancer, which were all talents that I secretly craved to possess. I was, for some strange reason, deeply humiliated by the fact that I wasn't accomplished in these ways. Since I didn't think that skinny and smart were enough to ever really be interesting, I learned to compensate by keeping busy.

Though I wasn't aware of my internal agenda at the time, I now realize that I desperately needed to fill my plate with interesting experiences so that I would always have interesting things to talk about and, therefore, could hide the fact that I felt like an inherently uninteresting person.

It turned out that I was indeed very talented at keeping busy.

By my senior year of high school, I was an A student, a class officer, a founder of an afterschool club. I also had a part-time job, attended religious school (albeit involuntarily), and was in charge of planning the prom. I was a Kiltie, which was a cheerleader-type kick line, but mostly we walked around school wearing little kilts, pom poms, and cool black coats.

Despite my frenetic pace, I was always competent, cool and calm (at least on the outside). It was around that time that I started having what I call "mystery ailments."

My first mystery ailment was restless legs for many years. Then, at fourteen, came a case of bad hives that lasted for two years. At sixteen years old, on came excruciatingly painful stomachaches accompanied with violent vomiting that lasted, on and off, for a couple of years as well.

Every time the stomachaches happened (which I can now say were worse than childbirth), my parents would rush me to the emergency room fearing my appendix was on the verge of rupturing.

After hours in the ER each time, I was sent home with only unanswered questions. Since all I ever heard from my parents and doctors was, "It's only stress," I just kept my crazy pace going. I could handle stress. Busy was my norm.

By the end of my senior year of college, I was attending school full time, simultaneously working three part-time jobs (totaling forty hours a week), and auditing a class for fun at another college nearby. On the side, I created crafty clothing accessories with my roommate that we would sell at trade shows. I wasn't skinny anymore but I did finally have a talent. Nobody could do "busy" like me.

Looking back, I was INSANE. But, in some strange way, it was the only way for me to stay SANE. Feeling the "I'm not interesting enough" feelings would have been just too painful, and practicing to become a superwoman turned out to come in handy in the life that loomed ahead of me.

At 23, equipped with one year of "regular" job experience and years of my own superwoman training, I co-founded a technology company with my then boyfriend, now husband.

We worked over eighty hours per week and I quickly learned everything I could about marketing, sales, accounting, hiring, facilities, event planning, public speaking, contract negotiation, business strategy, and employee management to name a few.

Rather than drugs or alcohol, which, frankly, I didn't have time for, FOOD became my comfort drug of choice. My appetite grew and grew and for the first time since the "freshman twenty," my weight became a source of stress for me. I didn't, however, have the time or energy to do anything about it. **I was too damn busy.**

Together, my husband and I ran our bootstrapped company in the days when startups were not cool. Then, nobody could understand why two kids in their twenties would sacrifice travel, bar hopping with friends, summer shares at the beach, and all the other forms of twenty-something fun in order to work all the time. We were focused and driven and quitting was never an option.

The stress was relentless.

Because we were both at the office all the time, we ate three unhealthy meals every day:

Breakfast was a chocolate croissant and orange juice. Lunch was either pizza or some other takeout option at my desk. Dinner was often a pint of Ben & Jerry's Phish Food ice cream with two spoons. Every evening we would collapse into bed and then get up in the morning and do it all over again the next day.

On the outside, I had officially become a superwoman—smart, uber-competent, and tough. On the inside, however, I was a miserable mess. I had no time for fun, no time for friends, and absolutely no time for me. **I was so tired.** Looking back, I know I was very depressed and exhausted though, at the time, I didn't have time to figure that out.

Never one to quit, I kept going and going.

"Suck it up," I told myself. "Nothing you are feeling is real, it's just stress. You can handle stress." It was my mantra.

I kept up at this rate for years, and then I had a baby. My body was so depleted that I couldn't even make enough breast milk to feed her. The doctor noted "failure to thrive" in her file, but it probably should have been noted in my file as well. I was exhausted, lonely, and feeling completely inadequate as a new mother.

I took my maternity leave and rushed back to work where I could hide from my maternal insecurities. Although motherhood inspired me to cut back my hours a bit, I was always thinking about the baby while I was at work and was always thinking about work when I was with my baby. I couldn't win.

All day, every day, I would hear the critic in my head saying, "Why can't you make it work? You have total flexibility and you still can't make it work! You SUCK." I had no boss or mentor or friend that could help me steer my Titanic. I was on my own.

A few fast years later, I had a second baby and we moved into our first house. My baby was just two months old and my first born was in her terrible twos when we signed the papers and moved in.

My superwoman multitasking skills came in quite handy as I simultaneously nursed my newborn son, pointed instructions to two hired college students who were helping to unpack our moving boxes, negotiated a client contract on the phone, all while my two year old daughter played by my side. Multi-tasking at its finest.

But then, it happened.

One day, out of the blue, at 31 years old, **I collapsed. Literally.**

It was only a couple of days after we moved into our house when we packed up the kids and headed down to my parent's house in New York for my brother-in-law's nearby wedding. I was feeling an eerie sense of calm for the first time in months and I didn't know what to make of it.

As I was stuffing my mushy, postpartum body into my tight, black tie gown, my mom was helping my daughter get into her special new flower girl dress in the next room. I fastened my bracelet and slipped on my strappy sandals, when suddenly time started slowing down and I started feeling really weird.

It started with tingles going down my arm.
    Then my fingers went numb.
        Then my eyes couldn't see anything peripherally—only what
           was right in front of me—my pale reflection in the mirror.
           Everything felt blurry.
             Was I having a stroke??

Was I HAVING A STROKE?????

My mom rushed me to North Shore hospital while I cried hysterically. Sitting in the emergency room with mascara streaming down my cheeks and feeling ridiculous in my evening gown and perfect up-do, I sobbed.

I cried over being so scared. I cried over missing the wedding. I cried over ruining my daughter's flower girl opportunity. I cried over being an embarrassment to my husband and his family (who I assumed were rolling their eyes at the wedding over my poorly timed drama).

Pulling it together ever so slightly, I informed the emergency room resident of all the facts that I thought were important—I'd recently had a baby and moved into a new house.

After hours in the emergency room, hours of tears, a few neurologic tests, and periodic check-in visits from my supportive/freaked out/best man husband, the resident told me that my "symptoms were impossible for a woman my age and therefore, it was probably just stress."

With those simple words, he broke me.

I went home feeling terrified, embarrassed, and lost. I knew, in my gut, that this was not "just stress". My body felt alien. I started falling into a deep hole that would last two years and change my life forever. It was one of the darkest and loneliest periods of my life.

CHAPTER III

TAKING MATTERS INTO MY OWN HANDS

"We cannot solve our problems with the same thinking we used when we created them."
-Albert Einstein

For two years, I was experiencing daily repeats of this mini stroke-like episode again and again and again throughout the day. I started calling them wavy-gravys because I would get dizzy and feel like I was leaving my body.

I had a baby. I had a toddler. I had a fledgling business. I had a new house. I had a husband who was still working eighty hours a week. I was a mess.

What I didn't have was a support system or answers.

I started having frequent panic attacks and developed daily tension headaches from not knowing what was wrong with me. I was losing my mind. There were days I couldn't get out of bed and many weekends I spent lying on the couch with my babies by my side.

I knew that something was not right. In fact, I knew there was something really seriously wrong with my body. I knew there was something wrong with me. Inside, I was completely depressed, feeling insane and broken.

On the outside, no one would have ever known.

All my superwoman training had helped me suck it up and make it all look good from the outside. I kept up appearances. I was brought up to believe that keeping cool was a strength and getting emotional was a weakness, so I never let on to people what I was going through. I got caught up in a cycle. I kept going to doctors, describing my symptoms and their consistent recurrence, and they kept prescribing drugs, which I kept refusing to take.

Something in me didn't feel right about the prescription drugs. I preferred to try alternative therapies but nothing helped. Even my husband started thinking I was a little crazy. Although I was scared and my brain felt totally foggy, I was determined to find out what was wrong with me.

Finally, I did what any other Type A, resourceful, self-trained superwoman would do. I took matters into my own hands. My first step was to put on my detective cap and start doing my own research.

I started by interviewing my parents about the older generations of my family and learning their health histories. Then, I researched the drugs that the doctors were prescribing to figure out what they thought they were trying to treat. Since these were the days before Google, I read books—lots and lots and lots of books. I knew that my answers were out there and I was determined to find them.

Very quickly I started following clues and connecting dots, which led to following more clues to connecting more dots. I looked in my medicine cabinet to see the name of the drug on the bottle. It was Xanax. I had never heard of Xanax at the time. When I looked it up, I found that it was used to treat anxiety.

Why on Earth would a doctor give me something to treat anxiety?

It never occurred to me that I was an anxious person. I had always been so calm and cool on the outside. I guess I really had believed my own bullshit about being a superwoman.

Clearly this was why I had all these "stress ailments" growing up. Come to think of it, many of my family members were worriers. Oddly enough, the word anxiety had never once come up. What role did anxiety play in my "stroke-like incident"? I was perplexed.

Through my research, I tripped into some books that talked about migraines. I started learning about ocular migraines, which can cause many of the symptoms that I had experienced that terrible turning point night. I had never knowingly experienced a migraine so I knew very little about the subject and I read everything I could get my hands on.

I came across a book about migraines by Oliver Sacks. In one tiny sentence, it mentioned a rare condition that affects some teenagers where they experience violent stomachaches accompanied by violent vomiting! If this were a movie, the words would be shown with a light bulb and aura around them—bright and shining.

Holy shit! I had abdominal migraines as a teenager.

I'd followed my clues and found my answer some sixteen years later. My first medical mystery case was officially solved!

This discovery was one of the best discoveries of my life. I had an actual "cause" for one of my mystery ailments. I knew there were answers out there and my job was to find them. Now I was more determined than ever to continue my investigation.

Slowly, I peeled back the layers of the onion of my own health crisis and learned that my "stroke-like event" was caused by a combination of severe exhaustion, crippling anxiety, and this unknown predisposition to migraines. Something had to change. I needed a plan.

Now that I knew what was wrong with me, I needed to figure out how to make it stop happening and how to establish a new normal. I read everything I could from so-called experts about how to eat and live but nothing felt right for me. So instead, I just started paying attention to my own body.

I started to pay attention to how different foods made me feel and I realized that the foods that I had been eating my whole life were making me sick, anxious, and exhausted. I realized the importance of sleep and rest in my life. I figured out what exercises were right for my body. I paid attention to happiness, peace, and positive thinking in my life. And, over time, I created an understanding of what I, personally, needed to eat to thrive.

Once I started figuring all of this out, I slowly started changing my ways and amazing things began to happen. I no longer suffered from anxiety. I did not get migraines of any kind. I stopped struggling with my weight. Best of all, I learned that I am really happy and calm most of the time both on the outside AND on the inside.

You see, what I discovered was that finding happiness, health, and balance isn't about following someone else's diet plan. It's about finding out what truly nourishes me and then living my life on my terms. For years I was looking outside for all the answers but, in the end, I had the answers inside of me all along. All I had to do to get them was to listen to my body and learn to love myself for who I am, not for what I do.

As often is the case, our worst experiences usually teach us the best lessons.

I wrote this book for you so that you can find your own answers and receive the encouragement (I wish I'd had) to follow your own clues. I want this book to help you start to discover how good it feels when the pieces of your own healthy life puzzle come together and when you can begin to live the life of YOUR dreams.

> # "OUR WORST EXPERIENCES USUALLY TEACH US THE BEST LESSONS."
>
> —LISA LEWTAN

My husband and I went on to grow our little start-up business to be quite successful and ended up selling it eighteen years after we started it. Not only was this a huge stress reliever for me, but also it gave me the freedom to start pursuing other passions without worrying about how we were going to pay the mortgage.

I became a certified health coach, founded a healthy living coaching practice, and named my business **Healthy, Happy, and Hip**. Combining the information and the skills that I learned in school with my years of business experience gives me the unique ability to provide real, effective, and simple strategies for my clients that make an immediate impact on their lives.

Together, we set up food and lifestyle experiments so that they can gain their own insights into what their unique and particular body needs to thrive.

I coach them to ditch the stressful dieting mentality and to focus on long-term strategies rather than on short-term fixes.

I help them to discover how certain foods actually affect them so that they can eliminate what makes them feel bad and eat what makes them feel amazing most of the time.

My practice consists of one-on-one coaching, group programs, online programs, daylong retreats, and public speaking events. I'm also a blogger who shares honest, real (and sometimes embarrassing) stories with the wider world on The Huffington Post, Better after 50, MindBodyGreen, among other media outlets.

In this book, you'll learn how to break free from traditional ways of thinking about your mind and body and finally give yourself permission to eat healthy and feel amazing.

Assignment: What is Your Story?
Now that you know my story, take a few minutes and think about your own health story. This exercise is not about your experiences at school or work. It is about the messages, actions, and perceptions that happen in your body and got you where you find yourself today. Pay attention to what prompted you to buy this book. Start there and see what unfolds.

The Investigative Approach

SECTION II

CHAPTER IV

From Busy and Stressed to Food Obsessed

"It is not enough to be busy. So are the ants. The question is: What are we busy about?"

- Henry David Thoreau

Sometimes it feels like we are living life at such a fast pace that we don't even remember what it feels like to slow down.

We are super busy working, taking care of children, taking care of parents, shopping, running errands, looking for love, recovering from a past love, traveling, paying bills, staying up-to-date with world events, exercising, doing endless laundry, getting to the gym, going to school, reading, socializing, and keeping up with technology. We shuttle our kids to sports practices and music lessons and still find time to volunteer for community service projects. Boredom is not an option. We feel guilty saying, "NO."

Many of us get caught up in this pattern of overscheduling our families and ourselves. Your to-do list is your map. Your cell phone is your compass. We say we hate it yet we just keep doing it. We rarely give ourselves permission to sit down and reflect, think about our choices and our true desires, and schedule our lives with our dreams and long-term goals in mind.

Unless we get a thump on the head, usually in the form of illness or some other tragedy (like I did), it is the rare one among us that takes the time to look, notice, or analyze whether or not we need to be so busy or if we are simply using our busyness to avoid our real needs. So, we just keep going and going and going, getting more and more stressed along the way. Rather than slowing down, we turn to prescription drugs, wine, and food.

And, it is getting worse...

As we continue to advance technologically, we continue to find ways to be more "productive" than ever, while making ourselves more and more alone with our stress.

As of this moment, we can be reached 24/7 by phone, email, snail mail, texts, pagers, and virtually through nearly every social media app including Facebook, Snapchat, Skype, Twitter, Tumblr, Instagram, Pinterest, and more. And now, we can even be reached through our Apple watches!

What's so sad is that, in a time when we can be reached in a million ways at any time of the day or night, in any location around the world, we are more disconnected from each other than ever.

We used to have villages and communities to lean on, to be a part of, to share our experiences with, to celebrate the good times with and to help us get through the hard times. But today, as families move farther away from each other and we all get busier and busier, we become more reliant on doing it all ourselves. As we feel more and more pressure to be perfect, we often don't feel secure enough in our insecurities to open up and truly share with one another.

Superwomen are created...and they beget superwomen.

Some people look like they just work hard, then turn it off and play hard, but for most of us, we can't rest until the work is done and, of course, when you're a superwoman, the work is never done. Since the work is never done, we are experiencing a huge deficit in rest, joy, pleasure and fun.

So, instead, we think about food.
All of the time.
An obsession is born.

Assignment: Take a few minutes and think about what is keeping you busy in your life. Is it satisfying or draining? Now, do the same for your stress.

"SOMETIMES WE NEED TO DISCONNECT FROM TECHNOLOGY TO RECONNECT WITH LIFE."

-LISA LEWTAN

CHAPTER V

Do Women Think About Food the Way Men Think About Sex?

"I'm at the age where food has taken the place of sex in my life. In fact, I've just had a mirror put over my kitchen table."

-Rodney Dangerfield

As our to-do lists are getting longer and longer, we have more and more pressure to be superwomen at work, at home, in bed, and in our communities. Sadly, no matter how much we do, we still tend to beat ourselves up for not being good enough or smart enough or pretty enough or successful enough. We all have our "thing" we're too much or not enough of, and it does its best to make us feel crazy. When we feel crazy, we turn to food.

The more we turn to food, the more we start worrying about food. We worry that we are eating too much, that we are eating the wrong foods, that we are eating at the wrong times, and that we are eating for the wrong reasons. It becomes yet another thing at which we are "not good enough."

To make matters even more complicated, we are bombarded with messages from an early age that no matter how smart, accomplished, kind, compassionate, or talented we are, we must also look PERFECT. We must look like supermodels. We must be back in our skinny jeans weeks after giving birth. We must have perfect hair and perfect skin and a perfect body and never show signs of aging or stress. We can't have cellulite or wrinkles or chipped nails or even last year's style.

We get the message that there is something wrong with us if we eat, and we get the message that there's something really wrong with us when we have a big appetite. You know how people talk. "She eats like a bird" vs. "You eat like a guy." Talk about pressure!

We learn to hate our bodies for their imperfections and think that the only way to true happiness is to see a certain number on the scale. We fantasize that life would be perfect if only we looked like this or weighed that.

We also notice immediately if other women have gained weight or lost weight while we silently pray that nobody notices our own extra poundage. Of course, if someone doesn't notice those few pounds we've lost, we are demoralized and disappointed.

We diet. We stop dieting. We diet again. We try a new eating plan that we don't call a diet. We check out weight loss centers, sign up for boot camps, and live on juice or bars or shakes for periods of time. We fail. We feel demoralized and disappointed. We join a new gym. We hire a trainer. We stop for a donut on the way home from the work out.

The more we try to deprive ourselves of food in order to lose the weight, the more we start obsessing about food and diets. Many of us search for the one diet, the one health tip or the one medical trick that is going to work perfectly so that we can finally stop craving cookies. Then we get frustrated because we buy it, try it, and can't sustain it. We despair and feel we will never be able to get a grip on this "food issue."

Even when we know exactly what we are supposed to do, many of us have trouble actually doing it. This, in turn, stresses us out even more and that, in turn, makes us apt to eat more, hence the vicious cycle of suffering continues and we feel more and more alone and ashamed in our suffering.

We can't escape thinking about food. On any given day we are shopping for food, preparing food, packing food, cleaning up, cooking more food, driving thru, eating out, planning menus, hiring caterers, trying our hand at baking or doing our best to avoid the bakery.

For those of us who are food obsessed, much of our joy, pleasure, and fun is in talking about food, thinking about food, taking pictures of food, and eating food. Food, food, food, food, FOOD. This food obsession, dear friends, is taking up a lot of valuable real estate in our brains!

I have a theory. I think that many women think about food the way men think about sex. We have all seen those studies where they say that men think about sex every seven seconds or thousands of times per day. I don't know if those studies are true or not but most men I have asked agree that they think about sex A LOT! Yes, many women think about sex a lot too, but many women think about food even more. Some women even think about food while having sex. Why is this happening?

> "JUST LIKE MEN THINK ABOUT SEX ALL DAY LONG, I THINK THAT MANY WOMEN THINK ABOUT FOOD ALL DAY LONG."
>
> -LISA LEWTAN

My guess is that somewhere along the way, our wires got crossed and food became our go-to, easy-to-get, always available form of pleasure.

Traditionally, in our society, it has been the responsibility of women to figure out the food thing. We have had to think about food all the time simply to feed our families. We needed to determine what our tribe wanted to eat. We had to choose which recipe we wanted to follow. We had to buy the ingredients for the menu we planned. We had to prepare the food and cook it for others, not just ourselves, multiple times per day. We had to figure out what to do with the leftovers. Food HAD TO BE on our minds because it was our responsibility to figure the food thing out.

These days, however, we are thinking about food even more. Cooking shows are more popular than ever and cookbooks with beautiful food photographs are always on the bestsellers lists. But to really get a sense of what is going on with food, take a look at Instagram, Pinterest, Tumblr, and Facebook feeds and you will see food at its finest. Food, glorious food. Magnificent photos of everything from kale chips to ooey-gooey snickerdoodle chocolate pretzel stuffed brownies to sushi burritos! Is it any wonder that this is all referred to as Food Porn?

Just like watching porn works to excite its viewers to want more sex, food porn excites its viewers to want more food! As a result, we are thinking, planning, and dreaming about food all day long. Is it any wonder we are all food obsessed?

Unfortunately, the more we think about food, the more we want to eat it. No, it's not weakness. We are programmed to see food and want to eat it. It's a survival mechanism sewn into our DNA so that we don't starve in times of food scarcity. When food was actually scarce, this ability to eat anytime was probably a lifesaver, but now, everywhere we look food is calling to us saying EAT ME, EAT ME.

Fact is, there isn't a street you can drive down in any city that isn't strewn with billboards offering restaurants or fast food or ice cream. There isn't a magazine you can pick up, a show you can turn on, a conversation you can have where something to put in your mouth isn't mentioned. There isn't an airport that isn't filled with fifty versions of cake for breakfast or a drugstore that doesn't have rows of every candy bar you might crave right there at the checkout counter.

Since we can't change the culture around us so easily, we have to start with changing ourselves. We need to recognize what is going on around us and pay attention to how all of this food focus is impacting our psyches, our health, and our wellbeing. Once we can begin to do this effectively, we can also begin to find pleasure, peace, and fun in other ways.

And how about all this food shaming going on? We all seem to be getting more and more judgmental about other people's food choices. Just because some of us choose to eat meat while some of us prefer a vegan lifestyle doesn't mean that we are any better or any worse than anyone else. Because I coach others on how to eat better, people are shocked when I eat something that they wouldn't.

Assignment: Start Paying Attention

Start noticing conversations about food, pictures sent to you, billboards and commercials screaming at you, and how often you find yourself thinking about food throughout the day.

Before you eat something, think about what you truly desire and eat that particular food. If you are basing your decision of what to eat on something you just drove by, saw someone else eat, or were offered for free in the market, then that is not going to really satisfy you. It's like putting a Band-Aid on a sprained ankle. Those are all just temptations and will not truly do anything to really satisfy you. Focus on what you truly crave.

CHAPTER VI

Put On Your Detective Cap

"Your body can't talk, but it can send you messages through discomfort or food cravings that need to be decoded. If we acknowledge and accept our cravings, they will point us toward the foods and lifestyles we need."

-Joshua Rosenthal, Founder and Director of the Institute for Integrative Nutrition

Now that you are starting to notice what is going on all around you, it is time to start noticing what is going on inside of you as well. Let's imagine your appetite, health, and indeed, your whole life as a puzzle worth piecing together.

By following your own body's clues you will be able to connect the dots and figure out what is healthy for YOU. As we go through this journey, whenever I ask you to "put on your detective cap," I'm letting you know that there is an opportunity to listen and learn about yourself, your mind, and what your body needs to do to thrive.

When it comes down to it, there is no doctor, therapist, coach, or relative that will ever know you or your body better than you know it yourself.

Though I'm happy to guide you while you are reading this book, for optimal health, YOU will need to be your own best friend, biggest advocate, and personal health detective for lifelong success.

Whether you are trying to lose weight, improve your health, or just feel amazing, the first step is moving yourself up a few notches on the priority pole and to recognize all sorts of clues when they appear. I call this process the "Investigative Approach".

The Investigative Approach
The first step in the Investigative Approach is to start paying attention to clues everywhere so that we can get to the root cause of an issue. We will listen to our bodies, challenge our thought patterns, look to the animal kingdom, and take a birds eye view of everything going on in our life.

"WHEN IT COMES DOWN TO IT, THERE IS NO DOCTOR, THERAPIST, COACH, OR RELATIVE THAT WILL KNOW YOU OR YOUR BODY BETTER THAN YOU."

-LISA LEWTAN

We will also pay attention to:

Physical Clues:
- Cravings
- Aches and pains
- Bloating and cramps
- Brain fog
- Energy level
- Sleep quality
- Weight gain or loss
- Skin conditions
- Digestive issues

Mental Clues:
- Mood swings
- Anxiety and depression
- Fear
- Doubts
- Boredom
- Anger
- Happiness or sadness
- Insecurity
- Loneliness

To be successful with the Investigative Approach, we must ditch any judgment we ascribe to our self, to our thoughts, or to our behaviors. Instead, we must look objectively at all of our clues, symptoms, and habits as simply data. Data, or as I'll refer to them throughout this book, dots. I'll ask you to connect your dots and really learn to hear how your mind, body, and spirit are all communicating their specific needs and desires to you.

There is no room for shame or self-deprecation while using the Investigative Approach. All symptoms of weight, disease, and unhappiness are really just clues to solving the mystery of your own health and wellbeing puzzle. They're dots for you to connect.

Examples of the Investigative Approach
I use the Investigative Approach on a daily basis. Let's say I am craving a brownie. First, I slow down and try to get in touch with myself. I recognize that my need for that brownie is likely pointing at some other need I have in that moment.

What I might really need is a nap, a walk, or a hug. The presence of the craving for that brownie was the clue that my body needed something that makes it feel better. If I ate the brownie, I still would not be satisfied because I did not address my true need.

When using the Investigative Approach, rather than just treating the symptom (like eating the brownie), I try to look for the root cause underneath all the symptoms and solve the mystery of what the brownie may be Band-Aiding and address my body's true need.

Let's try another example:
Let's say you have a headache. Many would automatically reach for the medicine cabinet and treat the symptom. Using the Investigative Approach, the "headache" would be the clue to dig a little deeper. You might put on your detective cap and ask some simple questions:

Am I having caffeine withdrawal?
Are my eyes strained?
Am I dehydrated?
Am I stressed?

The Investigative Approach allows you to start connecting your dots and begin to understand your body and its needs in a whole new way.

Let's go through another example:

You realize that you are feeling particularly anxious. We have all been conditioned to find a way to get rid of the anxiety via medication or drugs & alcohol or yoga & meditation, but we are never taught to investigate why we are feeling anxiety in the first place. Sometimes there may be a situation causing our anxiety like a big event, but sometimes we can't pinpoint why this unrest is happening or what about this situation is so unsettling.

By putting on our detective cap, we can go deeper and ask:

Did I eat a lot of sugar yesterday?
        Did I not get enough sleep?
        Did I drink too much coffee?
        Am I stressing about something that I can't change?

When I used this Investigative Approach for my own anxiety, I actually uncovered a huge A-HA for myself.

"LIVING IN A NON-STOP CRAZY WORLD, WE HAVE ENDED UP LIVING IN OUR HEADS RATHER THAN IN OUR BODIES. AS A RESULT, WE ARE MISSING OUT ON VITAL CLUES TO OUR WELL-BEING."

-LISA LEWTAN

I realized that when I eat too much sugar, I worry more. I get crazy worried and ruminate about my kids, world peace, the headlines on the news, and anything else that's on my radar. When the sugar is out of my system, I am calm, calm, calm. I learned this, and everything I'll teach you in this book, by taking my own Investigative Approach with my own body.

By putting on our detective caps, asking questions, and paying attention to the answers without judging anything as good or bad, each of us can begin to connect our own dots and discover the source of our unrest. The telltale signs are evident in our own everyday eating and behavior patterns.

Using the Investigative Approach to Understand Your Own Needs
We need to use the Investigative Approach as a new way to look at our unique needs in terms of hunger, exercise, and rest. It is time to let go of the concept that there is one perfect diet or one perfect workout for everyone.

The most important lesson that I learned in my twenty year personal health journey combined with my work as a Healthy Living Strategist is this:

There is no one diet or lifestyle that works for everyone.

We all have different bodies, different ethnicities, different metabolisms, and different genetic profiles. We live in different climates, are different ages, and come from different cultural backgrounds.

Our hormones are different, our jobs are different, and our gut microbial ecosystems vary. Our stress levels vary, our sleep patterns vary, and our personal belief systems vary.

An Alaskan fisherman would probably not thrive on a raw vegan diet and a rice farmer would not be too happy with a plan that excludes grains.

Personally, I am not a fan of diet plans that stress me out by counting calories or points, making me weigh my food, or get really complicated with what to combine with what and when. Instead, I prefer to put on my detective cap and listen to my body, which is my laboratory, and experiment to figure out what works for me. I want you to do the same.

Become an expert at understanding your own body. Read, search on Google, investigate, and experiment with lots of expert advice. Remember, though, that you're the boss of all the experts and only you know what's right for YOU.

In my research, I have found that some experts will tell you that to be healthy, it is all about nutrients and chemistry.

Other experts will tell you that it is all about lifestyle and habits.

And still, other experts will tell you that it is all about understanding your emotions and triggers.

Well, in my experience and opinion, the only way to make lasting changes in your health requires you to address **ALL THREE OF THESE AREAS.**

To find a sustainable diet, mindset and lifestyle that is right for YOU, you need to pay attention to YOUR unique body and its particular needs. YOUR mind-body-health combination is unique to you and, just like a lock on your gym locker, quite different than anyone else's combination. While someone else's diet may work for a little while, following your own authentic food and life plan can unlock feeling good in your body for a lifetime.

Food for Thought:
Aren't you tired of trying
to follow diet plans designed
for someone else's body?

Later in the book I will teach you how to develop a daily breathing and/or meditation practice to help you quiet the chatter in your brain. For now, just try sitting still, closing your eyes and breathing deeply. Over time, this simple act will give you amazing clarity.

Personally, I know how hard this may be for some of you to actually do. If you're busy, stressed, and food obsessed, you are used to living in action mode. We live for the energy rush that gets us through every day. For many of us, the adrenaline rush is an unbeatable high.

Rest assured, there is no need to give that up. We just need to balance it with quiet, peace, time, and space for our inner voice to speak. We need to take time from living in our head, which is just ten percent of the wisdom available to us, and start living in our body, which is ninety percent of the wisdom we're made of. It's this ninety percent that we don't often tune in to that can tell us what's true and what works for our unique body.

Assignment: Learning to Listen
Find a quiet place and really tune in. Ask yourself, "What is not working in my body that needs addressing? Am I sluggish? Overweight? Underweight? Cranky? Bloated?" Write down what is going on in your body as you start to really dive into this book. This is just a snapshot in time that you can look back on later and reflect.

CHAPTER VII

LOOK INTO YOUR LIFE

"It may sound strange, but many women don't readily know what they love to do. Some of us have taken our cues from others for so long that we don't have much experience in listening to our own inner promptings about what we love."

-Abby Seixas, author of *Finding the Deep River Within*

Now that you are skilled in the Investigative Approach, the next step is to use it to take a look into your life. When you understand what is actually going on in your life, you may develop clues as to why you eat and live the way you do.

When thinking about our health, most of us will only consider our weight and fitness level, but our lives are made up of so much more. So many of my clients come to me to help them with food but it quickly becomes apparent that what they are really struggling with are other issues such as keeping their kids on track, sick parents, work stress, or other issues of daily life.

What if I told you that stressing about finances can cause tortilla chip cravings? Or how stifling your creativity can cause a brownie batter binge!

We often eat due to the stress issues in our lives, think our problem is food, and never get down to the heart of the matter. By using the Investigative Approach, we can look together, through our investigative lenses, to see what is really going on.

What's Really Going on with ME?

When I work with clients, we start by taking a look at their overall life. We consider the job, the home, the financial life, the creative life, the sex life, and so much more.

I start with questions like *Are you having enough fun in your life? Do you have creative outlets? Are you learning new things? Do you have meaningful relationships? Do you have a spiritual practice of any kind? Is sex something you enjoy or has it become a chore?*

Now it's your turn. Take a moment and really evaluate the questions on the "What's going on with ME?" worksheet that follows. What do you notice while filling this out?

(See next page)

WHAT'S GOING ON WITH ME?

Rate each area in your life with a 1, 2, or 3

1= This area sucks and is in desperate need of an overhaul.
2= This area is doing OK but could use some tweaks.
3= This area is freakin' amazing!

	Rating	Goal
I have plenty of fun in my life	1 2 3	
I have ways to regularly express my creativity	1 2 3	
My job (including being a mom) is going well	1 2 3	
I learn new things continually	1 2 3	
My closest relationships feel healthy	1 2 3	
I eat healthy foods most of the time	1 2 3	
I make time for tranquility	1 2 3	
Exercise is a regular part of my life	1 2 3	
I have used my stove in the last week	1 2 3	
I feel financially stable	1 2 3	
Sleep is a non-negotiable	1 2 3	
I have an active social life	1 2 3	
I am satisfied with my sex life	1 2 3	
Overall, my health is pretty good	1 2 3	
I have some form of a spiritual practice	1 2 3	
My clutter is under control	1 2 3	
I count on myself to feel happy	1 2 3	
I am pursuing at least one of my dreams	1 2 3	
I practice self-care	1 2 3	
Water is my drink of choice	1 2 3	
I like to jump out of my comfort zone	1 2 3	
I have clear purpose in my life	1 2 3	

First rate each statement with a 1, 2, or 3. Then a goal of THOSE STATEMENTS THAT HAVE #1 next to it. These are areas that badly need your attention. When our needs are not being met, we often turn to food to compensate

Are you seeing areas of your life that you have ignored? Are you already connecting some new dots?

When I do this exercise with my clients, the issues that come up are so widespread:

I realize that I'm eating in secret because my husband makes me feel...
Or,
I am eating non-stop because my job makes me feel...
Or,
I am eating Hershey bars because my clutter is making me feel...

Other clients discover that they use food or alcohol to calm down after a tough day. They're often in the thick of career building, raising kids, or caregiving for elderly parents.

Food for Thought: WHY are you eating most of the time?

Some of my clients are very social so they find that they're eating out all the time and they feel a kind of peer pressure to drink alcohol often to keep up in the company of their friends.

Some people I work with have really stressful jobs with no time for themselves and if they remember to eat at all, they're doing it on the run or making up for missing meals by eating a huge one at the end of the day just before they go to bed.

Others are dealing with illness and that's often compounded with a feeling of failure around how they use food and carry weight. And others, still, who can't stick to an exercise routine, hate to cook, or get frustrated with picky eaters in the house and just sort of give in to pizza or frozen food.

Once we put on our detective caps and identify the foundational life issues that are affecting our eating, we can come up with creative strategies to work with them and change our behavior patterns so that we can get the results that we really want.

Here are some client examples where we identified the issue and the results that ensued.

Ellen Snacked All Afternoon
Ellen realized that she was starved creatively. As an art minor in college, she had always considered the school's art studio her place to unwind and de-stress. Years later, as a busy working mom, Ellen was more concerned with deadlines and homework assignments than watercolor or acrylics.

During one of our early sessions, Ellen took a big picture look into her life and decided that she needed a creative outlet and was going to sign up for an art class one afternoon per week. Much to her surprise, unlike most days where she snacked continually, on the days that she was at the studio she never once thought about food. Ellen was able to connect the dots and determine that she was way hungrier for creative expression than any snack in her pantry.

> "WE OFTEN EAT DUE TO THE STRESS ISSUES IN OUR LIFE, THINKING OUR PROBLEM IS SIMPLY OUR BIG APPETITE."
>
> -LISA LEWTAN

Debra Mini-Binged at Midnight
Debra completed the assignment and immediately realized that she was not having enough fun in her life. Each night, she would sneak into the

kitchen for a mini-binge simply because it made her feel like a "bad girl," rather than the good girl she felt she had become. In her younger days, she loved to go out dancing and partying with her friends but felt like she was past that stage in her life.

In our session, we brainstormed ways that she could feel like a "bad girl" without involving food and realized that a weekly pole dancing class would do the trick just fine. By connecting her dots, Debra was able to easily trade a midnight eating habit for some active "bad girl" fun that made her feel incredibly sexy and alive.

Kathy Had a Take-Out Track Record
Kathy, a CEO with two boys and a husband, realized that she had gotten in the habit of take-out food for dinner each night because she was too exhausted to think about food preparation after a long day at work. Not only was this impacting her weight but also she was feeling guilty that she wasn't providing her family with the best nutrition possible. We brainstormed and came up with the idea of hiring someone to come cook a few meals at the family home.

At first, Kathy felt very uncomfortable with the idea. She grew up in a working class world and felt that hiring a cook would be a spoiled, "rich person" thing to do. Although Kathy had no issues with delegating projects at work, she struggled at home. Once she realized that she was already delegating tasks to others such as mowing her lawn or picking her son up from school, she was able to reframe her beliefs on hiring the help she needed and began to give her family the benefits of fresh, healthy dinners.

Ricki Needed Sweetness in Her Life
Ricki, an accountant, came to me wanting to keep accountable with her diet to lose a few pounds. Noticing that she was very, very thin already, I also learned that she was eating way too much sugar on a daily basis.

In our coaching sessions, I learned that she had recently given up soda, cigarettes and alcohol in order to be a good role model for her kids but was still hooked on sweets. I explained to Ricki that if she ate a simple, healthy meal rather than a candy bar at lunchtime, she would feel so much better, be treating her body with more respect, and eventually reduce her sugar cravings.

In desperation she sighed and said, "If I don't eat candy every day, what's left in life? I will have given up everything!" We talked about how other areas of her life might provide the sweetness and fulfillment that she was looking for but she wasn't interested in exploring anything deeper than the ice cream container. Needless to say, we did not make much progress.

The reason I am sharing Ricki's story with you is because it illustrates an important point. No matter who you enlist to help you in your life challenges, you are the one who is responsible for your own transformation. Coaches, teachers, and mentors can guide you, encourage you and teach you, but it is up to YOU to make it happen. Ricki was not willing put in the effort and, consequently, neither of us were satisfied with the results.

> "ONCE WE IDENTIFY OUR LIFE ISSUES THAT ARE AFFECTING OUR EATING, WE CAN CHANGE OUR BEHAVIOR PATTERNS AND GET THE RESULTS WE REALLY WANT."
>
> —LISA LEWTAN

Assignment: What Areas in Your Life Need More Attention?
Take a look at all the big areas of your life and pay attention to which
ones are not getting enough attention. Are you spiritually deprived?
Hating your job? Yearning for creative outlets? Based on the goals
from the previous worksheet, what dots can you connect in your own
life? How are these issues affecting your eating patterns?

Write down the top three issues that you think are affecting you and
let's take action RIGHT NOW. Call your friends and start finding a good
time for a girl's night out. Pick up the phone and book a massage. Plan
a date night. Get outside and go for a walk.

The more joy you add to your calendar, the more you have to look
forward to and the less you will crave food as a substitute.

CHAPTER VIII

Take a Sofa Safari

"Look deep into nature, and then you will understand everything better."

- Albert Einstein

Taking the time to put on our detective caps, to stop, and to really look and listen to what is going on in our bodies is crucial on our lifelong health journey. But most of us just don't do it until we get sick or collapse, as I did.

In my continued efforts to better understand my own body and behavior, I often turn to nature. I look for insight into our human drives, instincts, and habits, and then can better understand what the animal in me is supposed to be doing rather than what I have been told to do or learned to do in response to my busy, stressed, and food obsessed surroundings.

Did You Know...?

- When female baboons want male attention, they shake their booties in the air. Look at any YouTube video or go to a dance club and you will probably see many women doing the same thing.

- I once read about a zoo that was showing pandas "panda porn" in hopes that the panda bears would get aroused and procreate. Apparently, in a natural setting, animals see other animals having sex, get turned on and want sex too. In that second, I completely understood why we have a booming porn industry.

- There are countless stories of unfortunate hikers that have found themselves standing between a mama bear and her cub and are brutally killed. As mothers, we know that our job is to keep our children ALIVE. It's the same protective instinct that makes us grab our child's hand tightly as we cross the street.

Seeing how much we have in common with our animal cousins, it seemed only natural to me that I could find other ways to understand our human habits from observing more animals in nature. So I put on my detective cap and, right from my sofa, I investigated.

Here are a few things that I have observed and applied to my health philosophy:

Giraffes Don't Count Calories and Neither Should We
The whole concept of calorie counting will hopefully disappear soon. While I think it is very important to know what foods are calorie dense so that we can eat them in moderation, more and more studies are coming out showing just how ineffective, incorrect, and stressful calorie counting can be as a long-term strategy.

The times that I have counted calories in and out, I became a stressed out lunatic and felt like I was starving all the time. Do we want to live our lives by putting so much effort into calculating every bite? NO WAY! The goal is to put food in its proper place and relax about it. When we eat real food, found in nature, we can stop worrying about measurements and still manage our weight, all while still enjoying life.

Lions Do Interval Training and so Should We
Have you ever seen an animal in nature going out for a jog? Nope? Didn't think so.

Animals run really fast or rest. If there is food, they run to it. If there is danger, they run from it. Finding shelter or attracting a mate might get some activity too. This is a clue to me that our bodies were designed for interval training!

It's not complicated. Interval training is simply alternating bursts of intense activity with periods of rest or lighter activity, just like the lions. Walking with short bursts of speed. A spin class. A row class. Dancing. Just add bursts of intensity to any activity and follow it up with a period of rest and you are doing what nature intended.

Koala Bears Get Their Much Needed Sleep

Of course we can't (and don't want to) sleep most of the day like koala bears who sleep more than they are awake, but my point is that we NEED sleep to function. Most of us need around seven or eight hours but rarely get it. Lack of sleep will show up in some area of your life, and it's taking something away from you.

Food for Thought:
For those of you who say,
"I don't need much sleep,"
I would love to talk to you.
Are you drinking coffee all day long?
Are you thinking clearly?
Are you craving junk food?

Gorillas Know the Importance of Groups

Gorillas hang with other gorillas and together they eat, drink, and nap. Social connections are critical for our health. When life gets busy with work, children, and an endless to-do list, sometimes friend time is the first thing to go. Reconnect with your gorilla gang and make sure you have something on the calendar to look forward to together. It's good for your health!

Cheetahs Do Not Eat and Run at the Same Time

You may not eat while you are literally running. That's hard to do, but you are probably eating while doing other stressful tasks. Are you eating in the car? Are you eating while doing work or in front of the TV? Are you eating so fast that you can barely taste your food? Sadly, when we're eating while doing almost anything else, our bodies are in stress mode, just as if we were in danger.

We need to slow down to eat properly and mindfully. When we rest, we can properly digest. Instead of eating at our desks or on the fly, we achieve much better results if we take a real ten minute break and actually taste and enjoy our food.

Many Humans are Living in 24/7 Stress Mode
Watching animals in nature is a great way to witness "fight or flight" mode or what I refer to as stress mode. We, busy and stressed humans, are living in stress mode way too often.

Way back in caveman days, our stress mode response was designed to protect us against actual, physical threats like being chased by a predator. When danger was present, our bodies started releasing hormones into our bloodstream that would increase our heart rates, blood pressure, and energy levels. At the same time, other hormones enacted the release of more glucose into our bloodstream to give us more energy to flee.

> "WE NEED TO SLOW DOWN TO EAT PROPERLY AND MINDFULLY. WHEN WE REST, WE CAN PROPERLY DIGEST."
>
> -LISA LEWTAN

While all this activity was going on, all of the other body functions unnecessary to ward off the immediate threat of a predator, like proper digestion and immunity, would take a break during this (hopefully short) episode of mortal danger in order for us to focus on getting to safety.

While in this stress mode, our brain would tell the rest of our body to hold on to our fat for dear life because we didn't know when we would eat another meal. Digestion would slow down and fat storage would creep up in order to survive a potential famine.

Ideally, when the threat passed, everything returned to normal and our brain would tell our body that the coast was clear and non-essential body activities (like digestion and immunity) would resume. Pretty cool, right?

Don't Skip This Tip:
After eating, give your body a brief rest so that you can better digest.

Yes, stress mode served us well once upon a time, but today we live in stress mode all the time! Although we don't have the daily risks of living in the wild, our bodies don't know that. When we feel something our body perceives as a threat, like rushing to get somewhere, a deadline, a fight, eating fast, worrying, or even the thought process of beating ourselves up, our bodies go right back into stress mode and stay there.

In other words, our bodies are feeling under attack constantly and stress hormones are running rampant. Since we don't ever calm down, we don't give our bodies a chance to relax into a calm state of "normal."

Over time, not only will this make us stressed out, tired, cranky, unhealthy messes, but it can also make us put on weight or prevent us from losing those last five pounds of belly fat.

Assignment: Watch the National Geographic Channel
What can you learn from the animal kingdom that helps to better explain your own behavior? Watch some animal behavior on TV and see what you can learn about humans from observing!

CHAPTER IX

DON'T BELIEVE EVERYTHING YOU THINK

"The greatest weapon against stress is our ability to choose one thought over another."

- William James

Now that we've explored the power of our environment and our animal instincts, it is time for us to put on our detective caps and think about the power of our own thoughts.

We tend to believe the things we think, but the truth is that our thoughts are just thoughts. They don't exist as anything outside of thought land. Thoughts are not real.

We probably have 50,000 or more thoughts on any given day and we decide which are important and which are not. From the moment we wake up our brains are firing non-stop thought bullets like:

"Is it really time to get up? What's the weather? Will I make it in time? Where are my keys? I forgot to pay the rent! I hope there isn't traffic. I need coffee. Who am I kidding? I'm already stuck in traffic. What can I grab for breakfast? I'll grab a boiled egg and get in the car. I need more eggs. Aren't I sick of eggs yet? Why didn't he call? I hope I'm not getting sick from all the eggs that I'm eating. My nails are chipped. I need a manicure. I don't have time to get a manicure. I forgot to call my mom back. Did I forget to call my mom? Oh, man, I really miss my dad. I need a vacation. I wonder where I want to go on vacation. Yeah, right, I can't take time off for vacation. Where should I go for lunch today? Why is there so much laundry? Why am I the only one who knows how to do laundry around

here? What should I make for dinner? I need a job so I don't have to do all this laundry and make all these dinners! I need a housekeeper. Who can afford a housekeeper? I hate paying bills. Man, I look so fat."

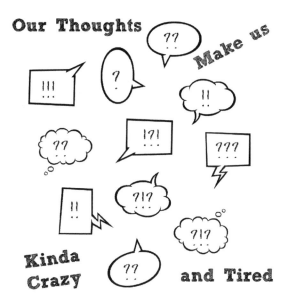

And this can be in the first few minutes of the morning! How exhausting! What is so interesting to me is that we can think all sorts of things that aren't actually true:

- *Just because I think it is raining outside doesn't mean that it actually is raining.*
- *Just because I think that I am lazy doesn't mean that I am actually lazy.*
- *Just because I think I am hungry doesn't mean that I am actually hungry.*

Get it?

Once we stop believing our thoughts and start observing our thoughts a whole new world can open up for us. We can stop attaching ourselves to thoughts that don't matter and challenge our limiting beliefs.

Limiting beliefs are constructs we have made up somewhere along the way that we use to make ourselves feel bad and play small. Here are some examples of limiting beliefs:

- *I am selfish if I spend time taking care of myself instead of others.*
- *I have always been overweight so I am destined to be overweight forever.*
- *I am only worthy of love if I am a size smaller than I am right now.*
- *I am just not a happy person.*

"ONCE WE STOP BELIEVING OUR THOUGHTS AND START OBSERVING OUR THOUGHTS, WE CAN STOP ATTACHING OURSELVES TO THOSE THAT DON'T MATTER AND CHALLENGE OUR LIMITING BELIEFS."

-LISA LEWTAN

It's time to challenge and release each and every one of the thoughts and limiting beliefs that are not serving us. It's time to write a new story and to dump the baggage that is holding us back.

Think About it. Evaluate it. Then Release it.
Learning to observe and release our thoughts without making them mean anything is a huge game changer in all areas of our life. This "thought management" is an essential tool to help us better understand our own hunger and stress. Using it will allow us to develop a healthy relationship with food and eventually put an end to food obsession.

Simply thinking negative thoughts repeatedly reinforces the conviction of the thoughts and keeps our bodies in stress mode. Stress is not limited to external situations. Even our own self-critical thoughts can put us into stress mode. Every time you say the words, "I need to go on a diet," you are putting yourself right back into stress mode and setting yourself up for weight gain and pain.

Some of us can ruin our whole day because we are mad at ourselves for eating a cookie or having a second cocktail. We vow to be better tomorrow. We vow to starve for three days or to work out excessively to compensate. But sadly, IT DOESN'T WORK.

All it does is put us in stress mode and keep us locked in the never ending stress cycle.

Another Way to Be
There's another way of being that isn't busy, stressed, or food obsessed. It's calm, mindful, and at ease.

When we stop rushing around and allow for a sense of ease to arrive in our bodies, we can start listening to what is really going on inside ourselves and we can start trying to understand what our thoughts are actually telling us rather than what we "think" they are telling us.

When we eat in a relaxed state our bodies know that we are not in danger and our digestion functions better.

> "EVERY TIME YOU SAY THE WORDS, "I NEED TO GO ON A DIET," YOU ARE PUTTING YOURSELF RIGHT BACK INTO STRESS MODE AND SETTING YOURSELF UP FOR WEIGHT GAIN."
>
> -LISA LEWTAN

But sometimes, relaxing about food seems impossible. When I used to feel food obsessed, I would literally count the minutes or hours in my head until I could eat again. Not only that, but I would turn the afternoon between lunch and dinner into a continuous snack fest, heading to the kitchen again and again praying that I would just get full and stop wanting to eat.

Eventually, by dinnertime, I would be full but that didn't stop me from eating dinner too. I wanted to be at the table eating with my family!

Then, somewhere along the way, I figured out that hunger was not the cause, rather the symptom triggering my eat fest.

> "WHEN WE EAT IN A RELAXED STATE OUR BODIES KNOW THAT WE ARE NOT IN DANGER AND OUR DIGESTION FUNCTIONS BETTER."
>
> -LISA LEWTAN

Thinking about food all day long actually had nothing do with food at all. It was merely a symptom that something was way out of whack in my life and thinking about food had become my "go-to" escape.

> "OFTEN HUNGER IS NOT THE CAUSE, BUT RATHER THE SYMPTOM."
>
> -LISA LEWTAN

So What Do I Mean by Escape?
The fight or flight response served us really well in sabretooth tiger land, but today it's something we can experience just by thinking about things that fill us with overwhelming negative emotions. Sometimes we can't leave a situation physically, but the fight or flight impulse is so big that to get any break from it at all, we just mentally check out.

We all do it.

You know when you're tired, and you're talking to somebody on the phone, and after a while you just don't have the energy to hear any more so you check out and start reading emails?

Or you are lying in Savasana, the last pose at the end of a yoga class, and you start planning the rest of your day?

> "ANYTIME WE ARE NOT FULLY PRESENT IN A SITUATION, OUR MIND WILL TAKE FLIGHT AND FOR THOSE OF US WHO ARE FOOD OBSESSED, THE LANDING PAD IS USUALLY FOOD RELATED."
>
> -LISA LEWTAN

When I put on my detective cap and explored my afternoon eating pattern, I realized that I just needed a break. Not a snack. I needed a few minutes of air, a walk, a phone chat, or a meditation, but the easiest, most available, most tempting thing was FOOD.

Ever since my early days working crazy hours in our start-up business, I associated breaks with the need to eat. Every visit to the kitchen was simply my body screaming to me, "TAKE A FIVE MINUTE BREAK." But I didn't hear it. I wasn't listening. Instead I would eat and eat and never get full because I wasn't addressing my true hunger. The hunger for a break.

Assignment: Notice Your Impulse to Flee
Start noticing what you are doing when you notice you're in "fight or flight" mode. Are you bored and want to think about something else? Are you looking for a distraction? Are you tired? Angry? When you notice that you are fleeing, do you physically leave the room or do you mentally check out? Do you reach for food?

CHAPTER X

Play The Reframe Game

*"Nothing in life is to be feared, it is only to be understood.
Now is the time to understand more, so that we may fear less"*

- Madame Marie Curie

While on my journey with the Investigative Approach, I became more and more intrigued with the power of my thoughts and decided to experiment more with my mind. Instead of obsessing about how I was going to lose five pounds while still eating massive amounts of food, I decided, instead, to play the Reframe Game.

The Reframe Game is a way of shifting experiences and behaviors away from non-useful self-criticism toward positive health and healing.

A Positive Reframe
One day, for fun, I decided that I was going to act how I thought I would act if I was already five pounds thinner. I wanted to remember why I liked being that weight and I was wondering if it was worth the effort to get back there.

So, that day I didn't get on the scale. I didn't scrutinize my perimenopausal pooch in the mirror to see if it had changed shape since the day before. I didn't try on the old jeans in the back of the closet. Instead, I got out of bed, drank my hot water with fresh squeezed lemon, and ate a delicious, healthy breakfast just as I would if I was five pounds thinner.

I put on my workout clothes and admired how amazing I looked in the mirror. When I sat in my spin class I just knew that everyone was looking at me wondering how I looked so great and wanting to know my secrets. I worked out harder than usual that day because that was what it took to lose those five pesky pounds, and I drank all nine glasses of water because that had been the key to my miraculous five pound drop.

Later, I put on my Victoria's Secret lace cheekies that my teenage daughter made me buy instead of my suck-it-all-in underwear that I had picked out for myself. I ditched the oversized chunky sweater and went with a form fitting stretchy cotton top, which happened to look perfect with my skinny jeans and boots.

I ate healthy meals with minimal snacking simply because that is what I would be doing at that weight and I didn't crave sugar even once during the entire day.

I felt amazing.

With weight loss out of the way, I could finally think about things other than food. I was more productive with my work and in a great mood. I felt sexier, more beautiful, and more confident and it showed—even my husband noticed!

So what was different?

On the scale I weighed EXACTLY what I had weighed the day before when I was obsessing about how I was going to lose five pounds fast. It was only my ATTITUDE that had changed.

Did I need to lose those five pounds? Apparently NOT. I just had to lose the belief that I needed to lose five pounds and move on to feeling like I already had.

If you're waiting until you get to a certain weight before you start living, try experimenting with your thoughts and waking up five pounds thinner in your mind tomorrow. It's pretty awesome!

A Negative Reframe

Unfortunately our minds can also create situations that don't exist and work against us, as in the case with my client, Jillian.

Jillian went on a girl's spa trip with some college friends. On the airplane, Jillian's friend started talking about how she dreaded putting on a bathing suit because she was feeling so fat. Jillian listened to her friend earnestly. She had heard this complaint from many of her friends before and she had even complained of this fat feeling hundreds of times in her own life, but somehow this time felt different.

> "IF YOU ARE WAITING UNTIL YOU GET TO A CERTAIN WEIGHT BEFORE YOU START LIVING, TRY WAKING UP FIVE POUNDS THINNER IN YOUR MIND TOMORROW. I HAVE A FEELING YOU JUST MIGHT LIKE IT."
>
> -LISA LEWTAN

All of a sudden, Jillian realized that she **hadn't** been worried about how she looked in the bathing suit, but perhaps she **should** be worried.

After all, she was heavier than her friend who was complaining. She suddenly felt embarrassed that she wasn't more upset about it. In other words, she reframed her situation in a negative direction.

For the next few days, old thoughts of shame about her body resurfaced. Jillian felt self-conscious in her bathing suit, became tense around food, and berated herself for slipping away into a mentality from which she worked so hard to escape.

When she returned, we talked about the event and how contagious bad body image can be. Together, we worked through some strategies for helping Jillian keep hold of her healthy body image and productive thought patterns no matter how her friends were bullying themselves.

She left that coaching session armed with a strategic plan of moving conversations about body image off the table. She also committed to spending more time with friends who were interested in talking about topics other than feeling fat.

As she tuned in and really started paying attention to the everyday body image chatter around her, she could hear how toxic it was and chose not to partake anymore.

With that decision, she was able to reframe the situation in a positive direction and set herself free.

Anatomy of a Reframe
Unfortunately, Jillian wasn't the only one who picked up on other people's "stuff."

Kathy came into the office very distraught because her husband told her she looked fat. "At least that was what I heard," she offered.

Kathy recounted the story to me explaining that she was getting into her pajamas and caught a glimpse of herself in the mirror. Unlike the old days when a weekend of indulgence only tightened her rings and her jeans, these days she felt that the ice cream and other eating infractions were almost instantly apparent on her hips, belly and thighs. She gasped at her reflection, which caused her husband to turn around and look.

"He saw me in an unbelievably awkward, highly unattractive pose that highlighted my altered state," she sighed. "Put on a few?" he innocently asked, trying to understand the cause of the gasp. He was attempting empathy and connection, but she assumed that what he really meant was SHE LOOKED FAT!

Kathy told me that she panicked. How did this happen so FAST? How could she gain so much weight in just one weekend? Old feelings of fear and anxiety rushed through her body. Old strategies that never worked in the past seemed to make perfect sense then and there. Starvation. Harder workouts. Self-flagellation!

Together, in our session, we stopped the escalation of all these whirling thoughts, took some time out for deep breathing, and then began to slowly examine each piece and part of the weekend. We then looked for ways to reframe the "situation."

The truth was that her husband adored her and thought she was gorgeous at any size. It was Kathy's own fear that was triggering her reaction and her projections. She was afraid, that if he really saw what she saw when she was looking in the mirror, that he would find her unattractive and undesirable.

Once Kathy realized that this projection was her issue, rather than her husband's assessment, she felt much better. She gave herself a big hug and told herself that all will be okay without the need for drastic starvation measures. I assured her that we all have times that we eat too much or drink too much. We are human and life is not about perfect eating.

Then, we worked together to make a simple strategic plan where Kathy just got right back on track the next day and was, once again, happy with both her progress and her husband.

You Are Not Alone

I share these client stories with you because I want you to know that you are not alone. We all have those times when we misinterpret what someone says, when we get influenced by negative body-talk, and when we can psych ourselves up or out.

Playing the Reframe Game is not only fun but also life affirming. It puts you back in connection and communication with yourself and the people that you love instead of creating disconnection where it doesn't belong.

Assignment: Play Your Own Reframe Game

Take a minute to record any situations that could use a little reframing. Feel free to send me an email at Lisa@HealthyHappyandHip.com telling me all about it!

SECTION III

CHAPTER XI

HUNGER AND HABITS AND TRIGGERS, OH MY!

"With habits, we don't make decisions, we don't use self-control, we just do the thing we want ourselves to do - or that we don't want to do."

-Gretchen Rubin, author of *Better than Before: Mastering the Habits of Our Everyday Lives*

Now that you understand the messages that you are getting, the thoughts that are making you crazy, and what issues are going on in your life, it's time to use the Investigative Approach to better understand why you are actually putting everything in your mouth.

I believe that we eat for one of three reasons: **Hunger, Habit, or Trigger.**

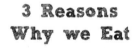

HUNGER

What does hunger feel like to you? Do you even remember? Do you get a rumble in your tummy? Do you notice if you feel hungry when you are upset? Do you experience a "hangry" (hungry/angry) state? Some people do and others do not, but it's true that many of us have learned to override our hunger awareness cues.

Healthy Cravings May Be a Clue

Craving a cookie is probably not a sign of hunger. Craving a bag of potato chips is probably not a sign of hunger either. However, if you are craving a piece of salmon with a salad, my guess is that you might be hungry. Notice I say "might" as opposed to "are" because we still have to put on our detective caps to better understand the clue and not assume anything.

When you notice you're craving healthy foods that are good for your body, see if you can tune in and pay attention to where you feel the hunger in your body. How do we even know when we are really hungry? I have noticed that when I am really hungry that I feel it in my belly. When I crave something sweet, I feel it in my mouth.

What we need, to make a difference in our health and our happiness, is some actual awareness around our cravings and our eating patterns. See if you can remember to ask yourself these questions when you notice you're hungry:

AM I REALLY HUNGRY?

What does hunger feel like to me?

How long ago did I eat?

What time of day is it?

What am I doing right now?

Is there something specific that I am craving?

Am I eating for a reason other than hunger?

HABIT

When we eat out of habit, we're engaging in some pattern of behavior that is conditioned. It's mid-morning and all of a sudden we're behaving like Pavlov's dogs, eating anything within reach just because we've trained ourselves to snack at 10:30am. We often tell ourselves that we're hungry when we are simply eating out of habit.

In fact, if I ate a scone every morning, I may start craving a scone every day at the same time. The good news is that if I replaced the scone with some strawberries every day, I would very quickly start craving the strawberries instead.

Sometimes we're eating nostalgically. Somewhere in our past we associated places, holidays, and other occasions with the foods we say we love and now each of us has a hard time imagining a menu change or a behavior change in many of these situations.

This is because we've associated memories, often good ones, to particular foods, specific places, or happy times. I automatically start craving lobster rolls when I hear the destination is Maine or matzo ball soup when I go to my mom's house.

We may even compound our eating with feeling guilty if we don't keep up with certain eating traditions. If we tune in and listen, we might hear these thoughts in our heads: *How can I not eat pecan pie on Thanksgiving? Auntie Lily will be sad if I don't eat her famous rice dish! A birthday without cake?*

I am not asking you to change your traditions, but I am asking you to use the Investigative Approach to question your eating traditions and see if you are eating these foods out of habit or nostalgia, or if you really want them and love them.

Eat what you truly want to eat rather than eating it because it will upset Grandma if you don't. When we eat foods that we don't really want to eat, they do not end up satisfying our hunger anyway. Eating out of guilt or "have to" isn't something we have to do as adults anymore, for anybody, for any reason.

Guiltless Conscious Indulgence

When you're hungry for what you truly desire, go for it without guilt. The trick is to know what you're eating and why you're eating it and, ultimately, that YOU **WANT** TO EAT IT from a place of conscious choice. So often we're really eating out of subliminal messaging and unconscious habit.

For example, let's suppose that every day, on the way home from work, you pass a frozen yogurt shop and suddenly find yourself craving a frozen yogurt. You stop and have one and find the next day that you are doing the same thing. By stopping again for yogurt, you're laying new neural pathways in your brain and this daily yogurt stop can quickly become a new habit.

If you find this happening, I recommend you try just taking another route for a couple of days before the habit becomes fixed and you find yourself stuck in a frozen yogurt routine.

Uncovering Unconscious Eating Habits

When I work with my clients, they come in with all sorts of struggles that they don't realize are just unconsciously conditioned habits. In our sessions, we work together to figure out what is really going on. I teach them how to self-analyze their eating habits in order to make optimal choices.

My client Lizzie, a master at personal investigation, sent me this email recently while on one of my programs, which demonstrates her ability to self-analyze:

> *Lizzie's Question:*
> *What would be so bad about doing the plan (that omits dairy) for the week but having cream in my coffee?*

Her Own Outstanding Answer:
You are either on the plan or you are not.

Lizzie's Question:
When did I develop this need to constantly chew something, gum, life savers, even carrots when I am not hungry at all?

Her Own Outstanding Answer:
Substitution for boredom? I really have to examine this one.

Lizzie's Question:
If one coffee didn't wake me up, why would three?

Her Own Outstanding Answer:
Habit, habit, habit.

Hilary, another client, realized that she always goes back for seconds. "I don't know why," she'd say when she told me story after story of always eating seconds. "Since I eat fast I'm never quite full when I'm done, but I don't think that's it because I actually start thinking about eating seconds while I'm still eating firsts."

In our session, we put on our detective caps and started asking questions. Did she need to feel stuffed to know when she was full? Or, was there a feeling of food scarcity from her childhood that was controlling her? If she didn't load up her plate time after time, was there some thought that she would not have enough to eat? "Is it that food has become just such a pleasure that I want it more, more, more? Why the urgency?" Hilary would ask aloud.

We discussed it at length and, in the end, Hilary declared, "I guess it is just a bad habit," so we created some strategies to help her let it go, including putting the food all the way away in Tupperware containers in the fridge before sitting at the table to eat. Just like that, with the awareness of what

*was actually going on and a strategy for success, the habit was broken and
Hilary stopped going back for seconds.*

What are Your Eating Habits? Worksheet
Put on your detective cap and in the list below, circle true or false to
indicate the things you do most of the time simply out of habit.

WHAT ARE YOUR EATING HABITS?
Circle each habit with a True or False

*(In some examples, replace the food listed with the actual food you
might crave. For example, at my parents' house I might crave a New York
bagel rather than lasagna.)*

1. I always go for seconds	True	False
2. I east just because food is there	True	False
3. At a beach town, I crave an ice cream cone	True	False
4. At my parents' house, I want lasagna	True	False
5. I eat until my plate is clean	True	False
6. If I go to Starbucks, I have to have a soy latte	True	False
7. I need to eat a lobster roll in Maine	True	False
8. At 2:00 I need a snack, no matter what I had for lunch	True	False
9. On my birthday, I must have birthday cake	True	False
10. On Valentine's Day, I want chocolates	True	False
11. On Easter, I need jellybeans	True	False
12. On Memorial Day, I have to have a burger	True	False
13. On Halloween, I go for the gummy worms	True	False
14. On Thanksgiving, I must have pie	True	False
15. On Chanukah, I crave potato pancakes	True	False
16. On Christmas, I live for holiday cookies	True	False

Maybe you notice some of the things you do out of habit that I left
off of this list? Take a moment and write them here.

Don't Skip This Tip:
If you LOVE it, EAT it and ENJOY it,
but don't bother if it is just
a habit and not a TRUE DESIRE.

> "LEARNING TO QUESTION THE REASON WHY YOU ARE CRAVING SOMETHING IS A GAME CHANGER."
>
> -LISA LEWTAN

TRIGGERS

Emotional Triggers are at work when we're eating to soothe or hide feelings in our body. We start eating when a certain emotion gets the better of us and we keep eating until we don't feel that feeling anymore. For some of us, that means eating until we are overstuffed and feeling sick or there is nothing left to eat.

Chemical Triggers are actual chemicals in foods that physically make it difficult for us to stop eating that particular food once we take the first bite. We think we lack willpower but, in actuality, these foods are loaded with ingredients that are quite addictive for some of us.

Assignment: What's Your Eating Style?

Before we delve deeper into triggers, I'm offering you a moment to start understanding how your eating patterns are affecting your daily diet. Start paying attention to your hunger, habits, and triggers.

Select true or false for each of the statements on the worksheet provided. Keep in mind, this is not a quiz. There is no score. It is a way for you to simply ask yourself some important questions and gain insight into YOUR personal eating style.

(view on next page)

WHAT'S YOUR EATING STYLE?
Circle each habit with a True or False

I eat too much food	True	False
I don't eat enough food	True	False
I eat when I am lonely	True	False
I can't resist sweets	True	False
I can't resist salty foods	True	False
I can't resist creamy foods	True	False
I don't like food at all	True	False
I eat really fast	True	False
I eat really slow	True	False
I reach for food mindlessly	True	False
I eat more when I am socializing	True	False
I eat when I am stressed or anxious	True	False
I eat when I am bored	True	False
I use food as a reward	True	False
I eat in front of the TV or computer	True	False
I eat in the car	True	False
I eat only when I am hungry	True	False
I graze all day rather than eat meals	True	False
I eat my kids leftovers	True	False
Once I start eating I can't stop	True	False
I snack often	True	False
I drink my calories	True	False
I don't eat breakfast often	True	False
Dinner is my biggest meal	True	False
I wake up starving	True	False
I wake up full	True	False
I know when I am full and stop eating	True	False
I do not feel full until I am stuffed	True	False
I am terrified of food	True	False

I would rather drink than eat	True	False
I eat at night after dinner	True	False
I eat a varied diet	True	False
I eat the same foods again and again	True	False
I eat in secret	True	False
I eat only alone	True	False
I eat what I want	True	False
I eat what I think I should	True	False
I eat when I'm hungry	True	False
I eat at set times	True	False

www.healthyhappyandhip.com

Now, take a look at all the things you have indicated are true. Maybe take a highlighter or, if you don't have one handy, just underline the statements that you want to be true going forward.

Please let go of any judgments you have about what you've indicated is true or false. Just let your evaluation be what it is. Now you have some dots you can begin to connect.

CHAPTER XII

THE RIGOR OF THE EMOTIONAL TRIGGER

"Life itself is the proper binge."

- Julia Child

It's important to keep that detective cap securely on our thinking heads when we're eating. When we're eating, you see, we're doing so much more than just eating. We're medicating our issues and looking for comfort from the friend we have in food.

Food loves to fill in as our lover, confidante, partner-in-crime, stress reliever, best friend, and pain reliever whenever needed. You don't even have to go looking for it. Food just automatically appears out of nowhere. For this reason, food has become the drug of choice for many of us. It certainly was for me for a long time.

Food is delicious and quite comforting, but when we eat for comfort rather than hunger, we usually end up beating ourselves up afterwards and feeling worse than when we started. What kind of best friend is that?

What are the ways you use food in your everyday life? Do you unwind with food? Escape with food? Run away with food? Put that detective hat on again and look at the ways you use food. Make a note of what you eat when you're not hungry.

Often times we think we are hungry but we are actually tired, stressed, or feeling bad in some way. Or maybe we're eating to celebrate. We eat when we're feeling good too!

When eating outside of mealtime, before you take the first bite, ask yourself, "What am I really hungry for? Is it food? A hug? A nap? Or a nutritious meal?"

What Time Is It? Watch Out for the Four O' Clock Villains
Emotional eating can happen all day long but it seems to start for many of us in the late afternoon or early evening. Something happens around 4:00pm when our willpower starts vanishing. For many of us, it is a downward slope for the rest of the day.

I used to find myself starving from 2:00pm - 6:00pm every day. I would continuously wander into the kitchen again and again to grab another snack after snack. By dinnertime I was stuffed but ate dinner anyway since I wanted to eat with the family. I did this for years!

Then I figured it out that afternoons were MY least favorite time in the day. I was usually alone in my house working and was a little lonely, a little tired, and very stressed about driving the kids to and from where they needed to be for their activities, making dinner, and then becoming the homework sergeant.

Since I tended to focus on my more interesting work in the morning when my brain was on fire, as well as run out for an exercise class (which was sometimes my only social time of the day), I left the more mundane tasks for the afternoon. What I discovered, through the Investigative Approach, was that what I really needed was a break, not another snack. I needed to stop working and do something fun for a few minutes. The superwoman, work-before-play part of me didn't quite grasp this concept so, instead, I reached for food.

For many of us in the superwomen tribe, the only time we allow ourselves to take a break is when we need to eat so we have started associating breaks with food. In our often high-powered work lives, it's totally acceptable to take coffee breaks, snack breaks, birthday cake breaks, happy hour breaks, but how guilty would we feel reading a book for 10 minutes in the middle of the business day when we have work to be done? Taking a nap, a walk, or calling a friend seems downright decadent in the workplace so, instead, we invent reasons to EAT.

What Are You Craving?
Paying attention will be the first step in breaking some bad habits that may be in place. Before grabbing food, take a deep breath and evaluate the situation as a detective cap wearing observer.

Becoming aware of what is really going on under the impulse to eat is the first step in changing your behavior. Pay attention to what you feel under the "hunger."

When we're tired, we need to rest, not eat. When we're bored, we need to do something we love and have a passion for. When we're frustrated, we need to express it rather than stuff it inside by eating. When we're stressed, there is something we're doing or thinking about or feeling that we need to face. And when we are happy, we could smile and dance and sing and jump for joy instead of eating birthday cake or Christmas cookies.

Eating may just be a distraction from us living life fully. And don't get me started on the whole, "I deserve a treat," concept!

> "FOR MANY OF US, THE ONLY TIME WE ALLOW OURSELVES A BREAK IS WHEN WE NEED TO EAT, SO WE HAVE STARTED ASSOCIATING BREAKS WITH FOOD."
>
> -LISA LEWTAN

Under all this eating are your clues, your dots to connect using the Investigative Approach. Maybe a real best friend is what is needed or talking through issues and going for long walks or taking up some long-time desire to start making a difference in someone else's world is what we're ready for. All this can be discovered as soon as we stop coating the feelings with food and actually feel the feelings underneath the eating.

Food for Thought
See if you can be aware of when you're eating due to an emotional trigger. When you experience your various emotions and you find yourself eating, what, exactly, are you putting in your mouth? Is it crunchy? Mushy? Loud? Does it dissolve in your mouth? Is it creamy? Salty? Silent?

When we notice we're eating and then consciously choose to keep eating, we can tune into the eating experience we desire and make substitutes. Instead of grabbing potato chips, a big fat carrot will still give you a crunchy, loud eating experience that some of us desperately want when we are stressed. You can even find crinkle cut carrots that give you a potato chip texture. Chia pudding can give us that creamy sensation when we are craving the comfort of ice cream.

I personally need to do periodic check-ins to determine what makes me happy and satisfied so that I don't just turn to food. Not the big happies like going on vacation, but the little daily ones that really matter and make life sweet. Sure, there are the obvious things like hanging out with friends or watching my children do something kind, but what about the simple ways that I can make myself happy in the moment?

SOME OF THE THINGS I LOVE TO DO...

LEARNING NEW THINGS ALL THE TIME. CURLING UP WITH A CUP OF TEA AND WATCHING A GOOD MOVIE THAT DOES NOT INVOLVE WEAPONS, MISSING CHILDREN, HAUNTED HOUSES, BLOOD, EPIC TALES, OR EXTRATERRESTRIAL ALIENS. GOING TO THE MARKET, ESPECIALLY WHEN THEY HAVE TASTING STATIONS ALL AROUND THE STORE. CHECKING OFF A BOX ON MY TO-DO LIST. DANCING, MEDITATING, AND LONG WALKS WITH GOOD CONVERSATIONALISTS. CREATIVE BRAINSTORMING, LAUGHING, AND STARING INTO MY HUSBAND'S EYES. CONNECTING FRIENDS WITH OTHER FRIENDS AND MAKING NEW FRIENDS IN RANDOM PLACES, LIKE ON AIRPLANES OR SUPERMARKET CHECKOUT LINES. GETTING INTO MY COZY BED AT NIGHT AND WIGGLING MY TOES. WEARING COMFY SWEATSHIRTS AND BLACK EDGY WEDGE BOOTS AND SHINY RED LIP GLOSS. WALKING AROUND A SWEATY CITY ON A HOT SUMMER DAY IN AN EFFORTLESS SUNDRESS. OPENING A BRAND NEW PACK OF MAGIC MARKERS. REMEMBERING SOMEONE'S BIRTHDAY AND MAKING PEOPLE SMILE. HUGGING MY KIDS. EATING SALADS WITH FRESH FIGS AND AVOCADOS. DESIGNING FACEBOOK POSTS.

-LISA LEWTAN

If All of These Things Give Us Joy, Why Do We Turn to Food?

Why do we turn to food instead of the things that will get us closer to what we really need and love to do? I think it's because food is easy. It's always available and it only takes a few minutes for the fake feeling of satisfaction to make us feel like we've taken care of ourselves. Often, we are putting food in our mouths way before we think about what else we could do to make ourselves happy.

Sadly, the food fulfillment fades fast and we are left with the underlying feelings that surface and can't be satisfied until we do the real investigative work to increase our joy.

Assignment: What Brings You Joy?

It's time to make a list of some things that bring you joy on a daily basis. Start by going back to your last worksheet. Notice the areas of your life that have been ignored for too long and need some attention NOW.

If you love learning new things but haven't been doing that lately, you may want to download an informative book on tape, subscribe to an interesting podcast, or just read for a ten minute break. This may prove way more beneficial than that cookie.

If you find that you are not getting enough tranquility in your life, consider using that ten minute break to get outside in nature. Breathe deeply. Connect with yourself. Take a walk.

Take some time to really think about the activities that you love to find yourself engaged in. These are things you do where you lose track of time. You feel nourished when you take part in these activities and they leave you with more energy after you do them with no desire to take away from the joy of doing them by stopping to put food in your mouth.

Fitting the things you love into your daily life will make you happier and less interested in using food as your only pleasure. They might be simple little things like sitting by the fire or drinking a cup of herbal tea. Look at my list for inspiration but then think about what lights YOU up.

Once you have your list, tape it inside your cabinets, inside the fridge, inside your car. The next time you are hungry or find yourself mindlessly eating, you can look at this list and then consciously choose what will really feed your soul.

Post a picture of your list.

CHAPTER XIII

THE VIGOR OF THE CHEMICAL TRIGGER

"I can resist everything except temptation."

- Oscar Wilde

Have you ever started eating a food and haven't been able to stop? Happens to me all the time!

Recently I was out to lunch and had a bite of the freshly baked focaccia slab that came with my salad. Big mistake. Not only did I attack the entire loaf but I started eating my husband's and daughter's focaccia as well.

Is this because I have no willpower? You may think so but I don't believe too much in willpower. I honestly believe that willpower is for comic book superheroes. The ability to control oneself depends on so many factors beyond sheer determination.

Think about it. We would never ask an alcoholic to sit at a bar with no intention of drinking, yet many of us with a weakness for sugar are expected to say no to a dessert buffet. We need to understand ourselves as eaters and then create some strategies that set us up for success.

By putting on your detective cap and using the Investigative Approach, you can start categorizing your trigger foods in a new way. Here's the magic question:

Does something in this food, an ingredient, set me off so that I just want to keep eating and not stop?

Bread is a big trigger food for me and I know that if I have one bite of fresh baked bread that I will keep eating it until the waiter takes the basket away. How about you? Can you eat just a bite of homemade pasta or wild rice? Just one crunchy chip from the bag? One velvety piece of dark chocolate? One glass of French wine? Once piece of creamy cheese? One homemade cookie fresh from the oven?

Some people can. Many people cannot. Using the Investigative Approach, I realized that most of the time I cannot. So, just like I do with my clients, I developed some strategies. When designing a strategy for trigger foods, the first step is to understand yourself, without judgment, and to be prepared for any situation that may arise.

Often, we need to simply remove the trigger food, get away from the temptation for a little time to think and breathe, and then apply some good strategies for the moments when we'll be faced with these trigger foods again. This isn't willpower. This is knowing your triggers and planning. Planning takes place before the first bite.

Here's my plan: I start by taking a pause and I decide, consciously and without guilt, before the first bite, if I am willing to go down that path and be okay with myself when it leads me to that place of stuffed that makes me feel sick. Sometimes the answer is still YES and sometimes the answer is a clear and unequivocal NO.

When the answer is YES, I let myself enjoy the choice I've made. Should I beat myself up over eating the focaccia? Why bother! That won't do anything. Lesson learned. Move on. No guilt necessary.

When I know the answer is NO, I go back to my saying, "It's not that I can't have it, I just don't want it!" (Later on I will tell you about my official "PAUSE technique.")

The key to retraining your brain and cultivating new behaviors is to understand your triggers and, if possible, avoid those trigger foods most of the time or come up with strategies to avoid overeating them. Is this easy? No. But it's not hard either. It just takes practice.

Food for Thought:
Strategies for Success with Trigger Foods
If you love rice but can't control yourself at home,
then eat it when you are at a restaurant
where they serve a limited portion.

If you want one cookie,
wait until the rest of them are all gone
before eating yours or take it to go
and eat it far away from the other cookies.

If you love pasta but know you overdo it,
try experimenting with raw zucchini noodles.

If you keep reaching into the jar of nuts,
divide the jar into smaller portion sized bags.

Or, there's always this: just say NO, THANKS!

Some of the Big Chemical Triggers I Observe
While your body is different and likely has different responses to these foods than mine does, it's still valuable to take a look at these chemical trigger foods and really evaluate how they affect your health and wellbeing.

The big five trigger foods for me include:
- Sugar
- Artificial sweeteners
- Refined carbohydrates
- Cheese
- Alcohol

Sugar
Sugar has always been a big one for me and I love helping people reduce or remove the sugar in their life. I have longed to be that person who can eat one tiny square of dark chocolate and be completely satisfied but, in truth, I will keep going back for more until the bar or bag is all gone. Sugar affects me in ways that make me feel worried, anxious, and out of control.

Artificial Sweeteners
Artificial sweeteners are a really surprising trigger. We think we are satisfying our sweet tooth with them but since they are NOT real sugar, our brain (which is expecting real sugar and is NOT getting it) starts craving sugar even more. Even stevia, which is considered "natural" because it is derived from a plant, is so much sweeter than sugar that it keeps our sugar craving engines fired up and looking for more.

Refined Carbohydrates
For many of us, any foods made with flour can trigger us. Once we eat that first bite of pasta or warm bread, we are hosed. When we eat whole grains, even if we eat way too much, at least we will eventually get full, as opposed to when we eat baked goods that can make us feel hungrier. Baked goods are filled with sugar and flour and do not contain any fiber or nutrients to slow down the sugar absorption or fill us up. When we eat them, we get a sugar spike which brings us up and then crashing down, leaving us hungrier than before.

Cheese
Cheese is a surprising trigger for some people. It contains an opiate-like compound that can give some feelings of euphoria. This compound, found in milk, is designed to make calves want to drink their mother's

milk. When that milk is turned into cheese, which is much denser than milk, there is an abundance of the compound in it. Cheese feels so good to eat, it but it isn't good for those of us who can't eat it in moderation.

Alcohol

Not only is alcohol a huge trigger for many but also it is turning up everywhere, making it harder to resist. Alcohol is being offered at school functions, mommy groups, and sporting events like never before. Drinking alcohol lowers your resistance to eating other foods and can have a huge impact on your weight. Can you limit your alcohol consumption to one drink? Only you know the answer to that.

...And More

Of course there are many other foods that are hard to stop eating (like nuts or fruit) but only you can discover which foods are triggers for you. Then, you can come up with the strategies that will help you eat them in moderation—or not at all. Of course, my chemical trigger foods will be different from yours. You'll have to keep that detective cap on and notice what foods trigger you.

How I Discovered My Own Chemical Triggers

Years ago, I started my day with a big bowl of high fiber cereal sprinkled with berries, walnuts and skim milk. At the time, I thought I was eating the perfect breakfast for me.

I usually had to go back for a second bowl (okay, sometimes even a third) because the moment I started eating it, I was suddenly insatiable. I rationalized that it was healthy cereal and, since it was so high in fiber, it would have a zero calorie impact on me—kind of like celery.

By mid-morning I was hungry again and needed a big snack but assumed my spin class was to blame for this. Truthfully though, I was hungry all day long and just assumed I was a "hungry girl" with a bigger-than-normal-appetite, which, honestly, I was embarrassed about.

I longed to control my voracious appetite, thinking that then all my problems would be solved and I could stop thinking about how much I hated thinking about food all the time! I could stop being embarrassed by my hunger. In fact, I felt like there was something wrong with me because I didn't eat like a bird like many other women I knew.

Then, one random day, I was talking to a trainer at the gym and the topic of my appetite frustration slipped out.

"Try giving up gluten for a few days," he said.
"What? I don't have a gluten problem. I eat it all the time and I am perfectly fine," I adamantly replied.
"Just try it," he said. So, I did.

Within three days, one breakfast was enough, my ravenous hunger was gone, and I often didn't need a morning snack even after spin class. Crazy, right?

Turns out that, for me, gluten is a chemical trigger food. When I have one bite, I am hosed. Eating what I thought (at the time) was good for me was actually ruining my day and my pants size. After that experiment, I put on my detective cap and asked these questions:

Am I allergic to gluten? NO.
Am I sensitive to gluten? YES.
Do I still eat gluten? SOMETIMES.

So I still eat gluten when I choose to, **but only sometimes**. This is important. Simply moving gluten from my "everyday" food list to my "sometimes" food list had a monumental effect on my health.

This list is something I often recommend. Just move the foods you love but know are not good for you to your "sometimes" list. Put the foods that are good for you and help you feel GREAT on your "everyday" list. Unless you are allergic, sensitive or triggered by it, there's no need to put any food on your never list. (Though I do put soda on the never list... more to come on that!)

When we work with these lists, we don't have to feel deprived like we do on strict diets and rigid food plans. For me, sugar is such a high trigger food that I have to keep it in a special "rarely" category.

Assignment: What Are Your Trigger Foods?
Start noticing the foods that once you start, you can't stop eating. Is it the sweet foods like chocolate chip cookies or Swedish fish? Or are you more into the chips and dips? Just start noticing for now. A few chapters ahead on our journey, we'll use the Investigative Approach to experiment with these foods for a bit and then REALLY start figuring it all out!

> "SIMPLY MOVING SOME FOODS FROM YOUR "EVERYDAY" LIST TO YOUR "SOMETIMES" LIST CAN BE MONUMENTAL."
>
> -LISA LEWTAN

CHAPTER XIII

ONE GIRL'S CUPCAKE IS ANOTHER GIRL'S CRACK COCAINE

"Some of the largest companies are now using brain scans to study how we react neurologically to certain foods, especially to sugar. They've discovered that the brain lights up for sugar the same way it does for cocaine."

- Michael Moss, author of *Salt Sugar Fat: How the Food Giants Hooked Us*

Sugar is a real tough one for many of us. Like a bad boyfriend, we keep vowing to break up, but something keeps bringing us back! Well, even after I broke up with sugar, I would be lying if I didn't admit that I am seduced back into its arms every so often.

At least now, when I do slip, I know how to get the sugar back out of my life without too much damage. I know that sugar is bad for my physically but, for me, the most insidious thing about sugar is the mental hold it has on me. It makes me crazy!

I remember the moment, years ago, when I made the exact food-mood connection with sugar. I was going out for ice cream with a group of new moms when my friend Ginger said, "Ice cream makes me feel sad." Not "fat," not "bloated," not "guilty." She said "sad."

This blew my mind.

A light bulb went off in my head. I had NEVER made any food-mood connection before and I KNEW from that moment that what I had to look at was how every food affected my emotional state. I suspected that sugar was a culprit, but it took me years of trial and error to really understand the magnitude of its impact.

I Don't Worry About Sugar, I Worry Because of Sugar

Another great awakening about sugar and its effects on me came the day I ate half a big jar of raisinettes and subsequently had a major anxiety attack. It was time to put on my detective cap.

I tested out my *"sugar makes me crazy theory"* again and again and my findings were quite consistent. After eating too much sugar, I would get moody. I would get light headed. I would want to scream. Sometimes, I would even get the shakes.

The day after Halloween, in fact, I would turn into a full blown witch! It would always start off innocently enough. I'd sample a piece or two of my kids' Halloween candy and, in no time, end up with a pile of wrappers, a dizzy spell, and a friggin', *"Don't come near me or I will be forced to hurt you!"* sign emblazoned on my forehead.

Here is the most profound finding of all and it took me YEARS to make this connection:

When I eat sugar, I WORRY more. A lot more. I worry about people dying and getting hurt and planes crashing and terrorism. I get snippy and more self-critical. When I don't eat sugar, I am at peace.

Food for Thought

Stop and think about this for a few minutes.
Do you worry often?
Do you consider yourself to be anxious?
Did you ever consider that sugar
might be having this type of effect on you?

Sugar. Just a spoonful of sugar. This bit of candy coated feel good that we learn to love as children is not so innocent. This may be life changing for some of you. It absolutely was for me.

I do try to stay away from sugar as much as possible but when I do choose to indulge, and I still do from time to time, I don't beat myself up. I'm very, very wary of sugar and the way it affects me. It's deadly, really, so I treat it like the poison it is for me. Every time I do bring it back into my body, within a few days I clearly remember why I gave it up in the first place and begin the arduous task of getting it back out of my system again because I feel so awful living in what I call "the sugar zone!"

People don't always understand how serious staying away from sugar is for me.

In fact, last year, my friend emailed me to tell me that she wanted to make sure that our annual birthday lunch was extra special.

"Promise me you will eat a birthday cupcake with me this year," she pleaded in her email, clearly remembering that I had passed on it last year.

I know her intentions were innocent but as a person who helps people adopt healthy eating strategies for a living, I couldn't help but wonder why does she care what I eat? Why is she thinking about it six weeks in advance of our date? Why do we need to eat something sweet to make the day special? And how do I explain to her that it is not about calories or willpower, rather something far more distressing?

Remember, one girl's cupcake is another girl's crack cocaine.

As a former self-proclaimed birthday cake freak, I once took delight in all the important cake questions: My favorite bakery or homemade? Buttercream or fondant? Raspberry filling or mocha?

As if it were a painting in a museum, I admired the craftsmanship and artistry in the birthday cake's intricate design.

When the big day arrived, I pretended to care about the rest of the meal but all I could think about was that melt-in-your-mouth pink flower made entirely of red dye number five icing.

I would cut my piece carefully, ensuring that the frosting-to-cake ratio was the precisely right percentage and salivated as I anticipated the sweetness. When I took that first bite, it was as if crack cocaine had been injected into my bloodstream and it took me to a sugar high state of nirvana.

After a few more bites, my cake would have mysteriously evaporated and unfortunately, right on schedule, my downward spiral would begin.

Yes, I am a sugar addict.
Will it kill me? No.
Has it made me overweight? No.
Has it taken away from me having my amazing life? Absolutely not.

Then what is the big deal? You might ask. It is a HUGE deal for me and many of you, I suspect. Having paid attention to the consequences of this opiate seducing my body over the last twenty years, I can tell you that it affects me more than I had ever imagined.

The more sugar I eat, the more I sugar want.

The more of it I eat, the more anxious I get. The more anxious I get, the angrier I get and the more I let crushing self-doubt and self-criticism creep in.

The more sugar I eat, the more I get PMS and hot flashes.

The more sugar I eat, the more I think about ALL the things that might ever go wrong for any of the people I love.

The more sugar I eat, the more I think about ALL food all day long.

In other words, I feel horrible, get angry at the world, and yet all I want to do is eat more, more, more of it! **Then why on Earth do I then eat it? Frankly, I think it is because it just tastes so damn good.**

Kicking the Habit

I have given up sugar completely numerous times. It takes about two weeks to get it out of my system and then a beautiful, grounded, real euphoria comes over me. I smile more. I glow. I easily pass on dessert not because it is something that I "can't have" but because it is something that I don't want.

Getting through those two weeks is Hell and I have failed many attempts getting there, but when I succeed...ooh la la...I am one happy girl. I walk around smiling and feeling terrific.

BUT, then comes the proverbial "oops."

The gourmet chocolate on the hotel bed, the homemade ice cream on a hot summer day, or my birthday comes around again and my friends and family offer me what they know I once loved and it is time for me to stare down my nemesis, my birthday cake, and wonder, as if I were Hamlet, "To cake or not to cake?"

Are you seeing where I am going with this?

"IT'S NOT THAT I CAN'T HAVE IT, IT'S BECAUSE I DON'T WANT IT."

-LISA LEWTAN

I have experimented with the "*one square of dark chocolate every day*" approach and the "*eat a special dessert once a week so you don't feel deprived*" approach, and the "*artificial sweetener approach*," and the "*only eat unrefined sugar*" approach but sadly those strategies don't work for me. Sometimes "*everything in moderation*" just doesn't apply. Yes, it really sucks.

It Was A "Not to Cake" Year
When a different friend asked if she could bring me a birthday cake on my birthday, I paused and said, "*Not really interested, but thanks.*" My daughter offered to bake me a cake. I said, "*Aw... but no, thanks.*" My husband even came through and offered to pick up a cake from my favorite bakery thirty minutes away. "*Nope*," was my reply.

Truthfully, I was feeling pretty great that day and wanted to continue feeling that way.

And, you know what? Dreaming about birthday cake wasn't what I needed that day and it was my birthday after all so I thought I should get what I wanted...and this year, by some miracle of miracles, IT

WASN'T CAKE.

I don't know yet about next year.

And even though I've given you the long list of how I know sugar affects me, unfortunately that doesn't mean I'll never eat sugar again. So, yes, sometimes you will see me indulging in dessert and sometimes you will see me taking a pass because the sugar is out of my system. And if you do see me passing on dessert, please be happy for me and let me be.

It will be not because I have superhero willpower or want to make you feel bad, but because I am choosing to indulge in life rather than cake. And that, my friend, is what celebrating birthdays is all about.

Assignment: Sugar & You
What role is sugar playing in your life? Are you sugar sensitive? Many of us are and there is a huge group of people who are but don't know it! Do you need a little something sweet every day? Take a moment and think about it and record your thoughts.

> "TODAY I CHOOSE TO INDULGE
> IN LIFE RATHER THAN CAKE."
>
> -LISA LEWTAN

CHAPTER VX

ELIMINATE, INVESTIGATE, & ALLEVIATE

"Your body is not a bank account. It's a chemistry lab."

- JJ Virgin, author of *The Virgin Diet*

Through the Investigative Approach, I started to become more and more aware of how particular foods were affecting me. If sugar could make me anxious and gluten could make me hungry, I wondered what else was impacting me and how? Like I often do, I put on my detective cap and set up an experiment to isolate the effects of certain foods so I could better understand what eating them was doing to my mind and body.

The results were downright fascinating. The experience was life changing.

By eliminating gluten and dairy at the same time as the sugar, I found that it was easier for me to get the sugar out of my system than usual and that I found myself feeling particularly amazing. Very quickly, I felt physically lighter and emotionally clearer. In fact, I felt incredibly empowered.

With the surge of confidence I was feeling, I chose to quit chewing gum cold turkey. It sounds like a small thing, quitting gum, but before that point I had been chewing gum all day long and rationalized that it was helping me in some way. I chewed gum because I thought it was helping to keep me from eating other foods. Truth is, I was both messing up my jaw and conditioning my body to want to be chewing all day long! I gave up gum for good that day and have not chewed a piece since.

A few months later, I designed a similar seven day program for my clients, which helped them to eliminate gluten, dairy and sugar like I had done in my own laboratory. I added soy and alcohol to the elimination list as well. I called it Eat to Thrive and had the group focus on real food without artificial sweeteners or chemical ingredients and discouraged all things that came in a package.

The results were beyond what I could have imagined and each client's experience was unique. Various client feedback included that, after seven days on this elimination experiment, they experienced less bloating, less hunger, less joint pain, more mental clarity, better skin, clearer eyes, increased sex drive, weight loss, feelings of empowerment and increased happiness.

After completing Eat to Thrive, one client realized she reacted strongly to gluten and turned out to have celiac disease. She was able to get medical help and treatment. The elimination investigation helped in medically beneficial ways to alleviate her ailments associated with this disease.

Their eyes looked brighter, their skin looked younger and even if they lost no weight at all, their jeans were looking better on them and they were feeling better in them.

In the interest of full disclosure, I have also had a few participants report that they felt only a little difference. So much depends on what they were eating before the experiment and how closely they followed the plan.

Am I saying this is a miracle? No way. It is merely another tool for each of us to use while wearing our detective caps so that we can come to understand our own body and how it is trying to talk to us.

Do I recommend eating this way all the time? Absolutely not. Life is short and being too restrictive is not fun or particularly mentally healthy.

But taking one week to give your digestive system a break and to kick your cravings to the curb is downright exhilarating. Once you have the knowledge of how your body responds without these foods, you are better equipped to make decisions on how to best nourish yourself.

Having done the program on my own and then offering it to my clients as a group, I realized that having a support network of others to compare notes with and cheer you on is a huge help. Word got around, in part due to a really positive article about the program in The Boston Globe, and I found myself offering the program again and again.

> # "LIFE IS SHORT AND BEING TOO RESTRICTIVE IS NOT FUN OR PARTICULARLY MENTALLY HEALTHY."
>
> -LISA LEWTAN

Clients who had done the program once would come back and do it again as a tune-up after the holiday season or an extended period of not-so-healthy eating.

Face it. We all get off track from time to time (yes, even me), but knowing we have this little palette cleanser in our back pocket takes away angst. We know, once we've done it, that it only takes a few days to get back to feeling great.

How It Works:
In my Eat to Thrive program, I advise giving up dairy, sugar, gluten, soy, and alcohol for just one week. This is NOT a way to live, not a habit to form, not a diet, and not how it will always be. It's just seven days to take some foods out of regular rotation and add other foods in and notice how your body responds.

Remove:
Sugar
Dairy
Gluten
Soy
Alcohol
Processed Foods
Artificial Sweeteners

Keep or Add-In:
Fresh Organic Vegetables
Higher Quality Proteins
Healthy Fats
Fresh Organic Fruits
Beans, Nuts, and Seeds
Coffee (1-2 cups max)

There are many different reasons why these five foods we eliminate are questionable. All these foods cause inflammation in the body and some may affect you in odd ways. The goal is to find how specific foods impact

Food for Thought
By focusing on adding in, rather than taking out, we don't feel deprived.

your unique and particular body. When you get to the end of the week, you'll feel amazing and realize that it wasn't as hard as you thought it would be.

After you have cleaned out your body, you can bring back the foods you've taken this break from, one at a time, in order to pinpoint your particular triggers and sensitivities.

What Are We Eliminating and Why?
Let's jump into a better understanding of the foods we subtract so we can figure out what our body feels like before we add them back into our diet.

Think of this program like the palette cleanser when you're at a wine tasting. We have to do something to get your mouth and mind ready to receive the sensory data that comes from these foods. As I've told you, nobody knows the answer to the right way for you to eat but you.

Subtract Gluten
Gluten is mostly found in wheat, barley, and rye. It can also turn up in everything from soy sauce to pickles. People may eat gluten all the time and not have an allergy, but many people find that they may have sensitivity to it and did not know it.

Sensitivity can show up in many ways from weight gain, cravings, headaches, brain fog, mood issues, to sleep disturbance, pain, or digestive issues (to name a few). As I mentioned, I found that gluten actually made me hungrier.

Everyone says "we grew up on gluten", but it has been modified and processed so differently since then that it's not the same food it used to be.

Subtract Sugar

Sugar is everywhere. Years ago, when the fat-free craze started, fat-free food didn't taste so good so they added sugar and artificial sweeteners to all kinds of foods. Now, as a result, we've got a whole country full of people addicted to sugar.

Sugar can be found hiding in everything from bread to salad dressing to tomato sauce to salsa! Sugar is clearly a chemical trigger and, in my mind, a chemical addiction so you may go through a kind of withdrawal for a few days.

The only sugar you will be consuming this week is that in fresh fruit. Eat it and enjoy it but don't overdo it or you will struggle to reduce your cravings.

Subtract Soy

When it comes to soy, there is so much controversy. For every expert that will tell you it is a wonder food, there is another expert telling you it is highly dangerous. I say moderation is the key. Typically, I do not have a problem eating high quality soy like tofu, tempeh or edamame once in a while but, for this week, stay away!

In truth, we don't know when we're eating soy a lot of times. Soy isolates, soybean oil, and other soy derivatives are made from highly processed forms of soy and are found in so many foods (like protein bars, veggie burgers, and fake meats) and is also used in restaurants.

Subtract Dairy

Dairy is very controversial as well. When I looked to the animal kingdom in my own investigation, I found it troubling that we are the only species on the planet that eats dairy after the first year of life or from another animal. Furthermore, so much of our dairy supply is loaded with antibiotics that even organic milk has unnatural levels of sex hormones.

Cheese is dairy too. Although there's that euphoric ingredient in cheese that makes it hard to subtract from a daily diet, unlike sugar, people find it reasonably easy to skip the dairy. It's non-essential.

Food for Thought
Many of my clients have found coconut milk to be a great substitute for milk or cream in coffee. Have you tried it?

Many people find that when they cut out dairy that their skin clears up, bloating and digestive issues lessen, and belly fat slowly minimizes.

Subtract Alcohol
When we drink alcohol, we tend to forget about our hunger, habits, and triggers and just reach for whatever we feel like indulging in at the moment. For some people, alcohol is no big deal but, for others, it's a very big deal. Just like with any other sugar, some people have trouble limiting quantities.

We're not going to drink any alcohol this week. When giving up alcohol, many report that they are much more clearheaded (especially the next morning). People sleep better, have fewer hot flashes, and fight less with the people they love the most.

That's it for what we're letting go of. Then, it's just a game of ADD, ADD, ADD, ADD, ADD AND ADD.

What can you eat this week?
ADD lots of dark, leafy greens.
ADD lots of other organic vegetables.
ADD fruits in moderation.

ADD nuts, seeds and healthy fats
like avocado, olive oil, and coconut oil.
KEEP proteins like wild fish, organic poultry,
grass-fed beef, lamb, and pork (if you already eat them).
KEEP your caffeine and non-gluten
whole grains (like brown rice and quinoa).

How to Begin
Use this week as a wonderful opportunity to clean out your body, your pantry, and your clutter. Here's how to begin:

1) **Clean out Your Pantry**
Make your home a safe haven. Give away or throw away anything that will be difficult for you to resist during the week. Also take this time to remove anything that you know is a nutritional nightmare. If you are concerned about discarding foods that the rest of your family wants, have them hide those foods from you for the week or perhaps just deal with the grumpy fallout and upgrade the whole family.

Sometimes people feel like they're being wasteful by giving away or throwing away good food and, if you're one of them, remember that food shelters are thrilled to get food donations and the grocery store already got their money and they don't care what you do with what you bought at this point! The higher cost of healthcare can be factored in when considering what to throw away. If it isn't something that's going to help you thrive, it's too costly to keep in your kitchen cabinets!

2) **Go to the Market**
Stock up with vegetables, fruits, proteins, fats, and grains like oatmeal or quinoa (that don't contain gluten). Buy enough of them for a few days. Think simple. Buy fresh. Buy organic. This week, only eat the healthy things you enjoy. Focus on adding delicious, healthy, vibrant food. Buy the highest quality you can afford. Frozen veggies and seafood are good to have on hand too.

3) **Focus on Foods You Add in Rather than Take Out**

By focusing on ADDING healthy foods (instead of focusing on what you've eliminated from your diet), you not only feel full but also you do not feel deprived. This is a very effective tool when making lasting changes—to look at the panorama of all that you're getting vs. the myopic view of what you're giving up.

4) **Eat Real, Unprocessed Food, Ideally in Your Home, Prepared by YOU**

You never really know what you are getting at restaurants, even the supposedly healthy ones. Forget the shakes, the bars, and all the "diet" crap out there and go back to basics. Just cook simple healthy meals in your kitchen with things that grow up from the ground, are fished from the ocean, rivers and streams, or are cared for in the bright, wide open. There is nothing as delicious as a bite of a ripe summer tomato from the farm or a juicy peach right off a tree.

5) **Set Up Your Refrigerator the Way a Merchandiser Would Set up a Store Display**

We tend to reach for those things at eye level in the fridge. Put the healthiest choices right there and you will most likely grab them. When all the healthy things are hidden in a drawer, it is easy to skip them completely.

6) **Aim for Optimal Timing**

Breakfast jumpstarts our metabolism and is particularly important since it makes us less prone to cravings and more likely to maintain a healthy weight. We should be able to go four to five hours between meals if we have eaten a healthy meal in the morning. Most of the time, we are not hungry but eating due to a habit or trigger. Going too long without eating though usually causes us to overeat later.

7) **Keep a Journal**

This is not for calorie counting or portion control. This journal is to help you connect the dots and note how you are feeling. Are you sleeping better? How is your mood? Notice the changes over the week. Write down what you learn from your body about what it likes.

8) Consider an Accountability Buddy

Having someone cheer you on and hold you accountable can be a key to success. We all KNOW what to do but have trouble actually doing it. An accountability buddy will keep you motivated and on track.

9) Evaluate the Other Clutter in Your Life

Use this week to think about other things that can be removed from your life. Is that pile of magazines causing you grief? Chuck 'em! Are there people in your life that are continually bringing you down? It is time to weed that friendship garden!

10) Add More Joy

Make sure you're doing more of what you want to do in your life this week. Put on your detective cap and investigate what else you can add to your life that gives you more JOY. This might be the perfect week to get a massage, take up meditation, or meet a friend for a walk.

11) Breathe. Meditate. Be Still.

We all know that we need to slow down but for many of us this is tough. We are used to operating at full speed and don't really know how to switch gears. Simply closing your eyes and breathing deeply for one single minute is a great start.

12) Have Fun with It

I love to name my salads! One day it may be "The Green Goddess." The next could be "Green with Envy," "Green Eggs and Kale," or "I Dream of Greenie." By naming my salad, my lunch feels more like a special event and I enjoy it all the more.

Name Your Salad

Name your salads and send me pictures at
Lisa@HealthyHappyandHip.com
for the Healthy, Happy, and Hip Instagram feed!

Food Logging

Food logging is helpful in understanding how various foods impact our mood, energy, bloating, weight gain, and all the other things we experience on a daily basis.

We're not tracking calories here. Lots of programs will have you weigh and measure and portion and count. Not here! We are just building an awareness of what we're putting into our bodies and taking notes about how that makes us feel.

> "SET UP YOUR REFRIGERATOR THE WAY A MERCHANDISER WOULD SEP UP A STORE DISPLAY. WE TEND TO REACH FOR THOSE THINGS AT EYE LEVEL IN THE FRIDGE. PUT THE HEALTHIEST CHOICES RIGHT THERE AND YOU WILL MOST LIKELY GRAB THEM."
>
> -LISA LEWTAN

You might experience some resistance to keeping the ledger because you want to judge yourself "right" or "wrong," but that's not what this exercise or anything in this book is about. This is just about awareness and looking to see what can be seen. Put on your detective cap so that you can find the themes and patterns in your own life's diet the way it is now.

SAMPLE FOOD LOG

Date	What I Ate	Reason I Ate	How Do I Feel
October 12	I had an omelette with spinach, tomatoes, and onions and a slice of cantaloupe on the side.	It was time for breakfast and I was hungry	Great! Satisfied and full of energy. Perfect way to start the day!
October 12	I had a doughnut and an iced coffee with milk in it	I walked into the kitchen at work and it was sitting there and I couldn't resist	Felt great, at first from the sugar rush but then a bit later came crashing down and UGH
October 12	Had 2 slices of pizza and a small salad with dressing on the side	Lunch - fast and easy. I didn't have to make it and I could eat it at my desk	Feel gross and I don't know why. Thought it wasn't too bad but feel bloated and sick
October 12	Had take-out including Lo-Mein, Crispy Shrimp, General Tso's Chicken and Fried Rice	Dinner with the family. We LOVE Chinese food and I can pick it up on my way home	Feeling lethargic, puffy, and have a headache. My rings are tight and so are my jeans

This is a food log kept by my client, Lauren. It helped her start connecting dots in a big way. Notice that her first meal of the day left her feeling satisfied and full of energy, which is what we are hoping for from every meal. As the day went on, however, her choices seemed like good ideas in the moment but left Lauren feeling gross, lethargic, puffy, bloated, and sick.

> # "WHAT YOU EAT, WHY YOU EAT, WHEN YOU EAT, AND HOW YOU EAT CAN AFFECT YOUR MOOD IN A VERY PROFOUND WAY."
>
> -LISA LEWTAN

What to Expect this Week

You may come in strong Day 1, but Day 2 and Day 3 will be the hardest. By day 4, you will notice that you actually feel good and it gets better and better from there. If you tend to currently eat a lot of sugar, you may go through withdrawal that may include feeling sad. Or, you may have no issues. Everyone is different. Nothing is unusual. The key is to use this week as an opportunity to investigate your hunger, habits, and triggers.

Dealing with Sugar Cravings

As you now know, I have been dealing with my own internal cookie monster for years. I've found that there are many ways to help me be successful when I'm ready to get sugar back out of my life.

Here are seven things I do to deal with my sugar cravings:

1) Instead of Reaching for Sweet, Try Sour

Many times, after a meal, we crave something sweet. Try eating something sour instead like some lemon or a pickle and watch the craving disappear.

2) Get the Sweets Out of the House

We are prone to crave things we see so either give it away, have someone else hide it away, or throw it away! Make sure healthy fruits and vegetables are easily visible.

3) Eat Sweet Potatoes

Sweet potatoes are super healthy, filling, and delicious. They are naturally sweet and eating some with your main meal can help reduce sugar cravings later.

4) Explore the Vast World of Herbal Teas

Sometimes a cup of apple cinnamon tea, peppermint tea, or spicy ginger tea is a great way to end a meal when you are craving something sweet.

5) Beware of Sauce

Did you know that some barbecue sauce brands contain roughly the same amount of sugar as chocolate? Ketchup and tomato sauce can be culprits too. Check your ingredient labels.

6) Ditch the Fruit Juice

A glass of apple juice contains the same amount of sugar as a glass of Coke. Even green juices have high amounts of sugar in them. Eaten whole, with the fiber intact, most of us are able to metabolize the fructose in fruit. When the fiber is removed, in the case of juice, we're left with a whole heap of sugar that our system simply can't process. Some people have terrible digestive issues with all fructose, so pay close attention to how it affects you.

7) Focus on Other Areas of "Sweetness" in Your Life

Life should not be focused only on what you can and cannot eat. Get outside, spend time with people who make you feel good, read a good book, and use joy to sweeten your life rather than sugar.

Using a Mantra

Many people find that picking a mantra to say to themselves throughout the week is a very useful tool. A mantra is an easy phrase you can say over and over to encourage yourself to stay in the game.

Here are some examples:

> *I make the right food choices for me.*
> *The right foods give me energy.*
> *I choose actively. I choose wisely.*
> *I deserve to feel light, happy, and confident.*
> *I can do this.*
> *I deserve to feel great.*
> *I am mindful of my choices.*
> *I don't need sugar because I am sweet enough.*
> *I have a choice.*
> *Feeling good in my body will feel better than any food.*

Pick a mantra right now and write it here:

_____

Reintroducing Gluten, Dairy, and Soy

After seven days, it is time for you reintroduce the gluten, dairy, and soy—but just one food type at a time.

Choose the first food and begin to eat a normal portion of it for three days. Be sure that what you add back in contains only the food itself—no added sugars, preservatives, artificial flavors, etc. For example, when you are bringing back dairy, start with a plain yogurt as opposed to a yogurt with pre-added fruit in it.

After three days, take that food out again, give a day of rest, and then reintroduce another food for three days. This way you can track your body's response to each food group as you add it back into your daily diet.

Experiment #1: Gluten

Start by adding back the gluten. Some breads contain added sugars, corn syrup, and other ingredients so check the ingredients carefully! Ezekiel breads are a great place to begin.

Experiment #2: Dairy

When bringing back the dairy, try only plain yogurt, not sweetened. If you are using dairy in your coffee, read labels and make sure it's not a dairy "product" that contains artificial flavors, sweeteners, etc.

Experiment #3: Soy

Reintroduce organic tofu, tempeh, or edamame. Avoid processed soy in foods and oils whenever possible.

Experiment #4: Sugar and Alcohol

Unlike gluten, dairy, and soy, take your time reintroducing your sugar and alcohol. You may feel so good that you decide to keep them out of your system for a bit longer.

If you do choose to add sugar and alcohol back, I recommend adding them back with caution since the cravings will return instantly. For some people, they can have a glass of wine and it's not a big deal. For others, it leads to a drink or two every night. Know yourself. Is this an issue for you? If it is, treat it like sugar. If not, once in a while is fine. Alcohol and sugar can be huge triggers for some people and make it difficult to control eating behaviors. Remember that sugar is highly addictive!

Notice Everything

Pay attention to your body's reactions to these foods. If you notice any sensitivity, stop eating that food or move it from the "*I eat it often*" category to the "*I eat it once in a while*" category. Give your body a day or so to recover and then try a different food group.

Notice any body or mood changes, resurgences of craving, or fluid retention when you add back these foods. Do you need more Kleenex than usual because you are congested? Are you getting headaches or experiencing a kind of brain fog? What's going on with your moods? Are you getting along with your loved ones? Can you sleep at night? Do you feel tired all the time? What about aches and pains in your joints? Are you breaking out? Do you have a rash or other itchy patches on your skin? Are you gassy? Constipated?

> *The other day I mentioned to my teenage*
> *daughter that, for the first time in a long time,*
> *my nose was running. She asked, "Have you been eating*
> *dairy lately?" I smiled and replied, "I've taught you well, Grasshopper!"*

Try and notice these "symptoms" as they arise in relationship to the foods you've reintroduced to your diet. Put on your detective cap and pay attention!

Go for Quality
Going forward, think about the quality of the food you are adding back. For example, if you want to eat bread then seek out the best quality bread filled with whole grains and no chemicals, additives, or preservatives.

Don't Skip This Tip!
Sprouted grain breads are a great choice since they use the actual grain rather than flour.

For dairy, look for grass-fed butter, cheeses, goat and sheep cheese, yogurts, and other dairy products marked organic.

This experiment is one you can do on your own but if you would like additional support, I also offer small group programs and online courses that provide more instruction and guidance to assist you in

being successful. Be sure to become a subscriber on my website www.
healthyhappyandhip.com where you'll receive the latest updates on
course offerings and group support.

Assignment: Connect the Food Dots
How did you feel when you took the foods out? How did you feel when
you brought them back in? Write down your experience so that when
you are not feeling your best you can review your notes and remember
how quickly you felt great when you were Eating to Thrive!

SECTION III

CHAPTER XVI

Fueling Your Internal Ferrari

"While weight loss is important, what's more important is the quality of food you put into your body—food is information that quickly changes your metabolism and genes."

- Dr. Mark Hyman, author of *The Blood Sugar Solution*

Once you complete the Eat to Thrive program and discover the effects of a particular food, you may still choose to eat it when you really want it but you will be aware of how it is affecting your body and your mind.

As I mentioned, I recommend just moving certain foods from the MORE OFTEN category to the LESS OFTEN category in your organizing mind. For example, if you love cheese but found it really causes you to bloat, you may choose to not include it in your daily salad, rather have it for a once in a while treat.

Many of us assume that that if we could just stay away from ALL food completely, we would solve all of our food issues. But we can't. We have to eat to survive and, frankly, eating can be one of our greatest pleasures in life.

The good news is that you CAN learn to relax around food (assuming it is actually food and not a food-like product or a treat). When we eat real food, we bring good nutrition into our body, engage our senses, and eventually get full. If we eat enough real food, then we are less hungry later with more time and brainpower to add in the things that bring us joy. On the other hand, when we eat fake food or treats, we want to eat more and more and never get full until we don't feel well or it's all gone. We return to that food obsessed state that keeps us stressed.

So what exactly is "real" food? I define real food as something that could be eaten without other ingredients added to it.

Think vegetables, fruit, nuts and seeds, legumes, whole grains, and high quality animal proteins like fish, poultry, or beef. They may be prepared to taste better with other ingredients but they were not created with other ingredients.

In each meal I like to have protein, fat, and carbohydrates. Personally, I like to eat most of my carbs in the forms of vegetables but also enjoy fruits and whole grains in moderation.

> "IF WE EAT TOO MUCH REAL FOOD, THEN WE GET FULL AND ARE LESS HUNGRY LATER. ON THE OTHER HAND, WHEN WE EAT FAKE FOOD OR TREATS, WE WANT TO EAT MORE AND MORE AND NEVER FEEL FULL."
>
> -LISA LEWTAN

To me, everything else is an optional food. Is bread a non-essential? Yup. Pasta? Yup. Wine? Yup. Cupcakes? Yup. Cheese? Yup. Do you hate me yet?

Does that mean we can't eat them if they are optional? Of course not! Just know what you are eating and why. Eat foods because your body wants them rather than thinking that your body needs them and plan accordingly. Please eat without judgment, just recognition. We're cultivating awareness here.

We don't have to eat optional foods every day, but there is no reason we can't have many of them over the course of the week. This is our life and our body so we get to choose!

You may be saying to yourself, "But my bread is healthy because it is made up of whole grains," and you are partially right. Most bread is made from flour, which I consider to be predigested grains. To get the best benefit, eat the grains directly, like in a bowl of oatmeal rather than taking in lots of unnecessary ingredients including preservatives, sugar, and those (in many cases) highly processed pulverized grains.

Try to avoid food-like-products. They can usually be found in the supermarket in a box or plastic container. These food-like-products are tricky. They look like food, pretend to be food, and are sold in a supermarket alongside food, but are really chemicals and crap in a package. Put your detective cap on and read ingredients!

Food for Thought

Have you ever noticed that certain popular American Cheese is not actually cheese? It is a "cheese product." Have you ever read the ingredients in non-dairy creamer? Reading nutrition labels can be quite eye opening.

Before you eat a bite of anything, ask yourself, "Am I bringing nutrition into my body or taking it out?" If you are taking it out, it is a treat. You can eat treats, you just have to turn down the frequency. That once-in-a-while-only list is an important one to help keep you on track.

How Does It Make Me Feel

Start looking at foods in terms of how they make you feel rather than labeling them good or bad and you will naturally gravitate to a healthier place. I love to do food experiments with my clients using the Investigative Approach. It absolutely always brings insights and awareness that they can use to make a difference in their everyday eating.

For example, in the snack experiment, we will try a different snack each day of the week and see which is the most satisfying in terms of satiety until dinner. For some, an apple and peanut butter is the way to go but for someone else, hard boiled eggs are unbeatable. By putting your detective cap on, it is amazing what you will learn!

Be a Food SNOB!

YES, be a food SNOB! Only eat the best quality, most delicious version of anything you eat. For example, if you want to eat chocolate, find the best organic, raw, dark, velvety chocolate you can find. If you want to eat pasta, go find the freshest pasta available, ideally homemade in a little village in Italy!

Focus on food quality rather than quantity. Spend your food budget on the best quality real food you enjoy. Eat the highest quality food you can afford. As soon as you start counting healthcare costs, you'll realize you can't afford not to.

The Chocolate Chip Cookie Story
Years ago, while hanging out at Miraval,
a spa in Arizona that I love which focuses on mindfulness,
I met a wise woman who shared a story with me
about taking her young son to the grocery store.
He pleaded, "Can we buy some chocolate chip cookies?"

"Maybe," she replied.
She then asked her son to count the number
of ingredients on the package of the cookies. There were twenty-three.

When she asked her son how many ingredients
they use at home to bake chocolate chip cookies,
he could only recall seven ingredients.
His mom explained that the mysterious other sixteen ingredients
were simply to increase the cookies' shelf life in the store.
Rather than buying the cookies,
they went home and baked.

After that conversation,
I started reading labels before buying
anything and am continually shocked at my findings.

RATHER THAN ASKING "HOW MANY CALORIES ARE IN
THIS FOOD?", ASK "IS THIS THE HIGHEST QUALITY,
MOST DELICIOUS, NUTRIENT-DENSE, FRESHEST, MOST
SATISYING, AND HEALTHFUL CHOICE THAT MY
BEAUTIFUL, ROCKSTAR, MIRACULOUS BODY DESERVES?" I
THINK YOU WILL MAKE THE BETTER CHOICE :)

www.HealthyHappyandHip.com

Premium Fuel
Picture a beautiful tomato vine growing outside in your garden. It is receiving nutrients from the earth below and the sun above. It is alive and thriving and shining in all of its glory. All that positive energy enters your body when you eat that glorious tomato.

Now think of the energy in a box of cereal that has been loaded up with preservatives so that it can sit on a shelf for two years. What energy is that giving to your body?

Put on your detective cap and look in the mirror. Ask yourself, which food does YOUR body deserve?

Now picture a Ferrari. Would you dream of giving it anything except premium fuel? Of course not. You are that Ferrari. You deserve the best fuel possible.

Some of us like to spend money on clothing and accessories, others are willing to spend on education. The best gift, however, that you can give to yourself and your family is health. The food you eat is one of the best health investments you can make. Sticking with real food is a safe bet.

Start Trusting When Something Does Not Make Sense to You
Years ago, avocados got a really bad reputation because they were calorie dense. Many people shunned avocados but inside I had a feeling that they were magical and good for me and I kept eating them. Today, avocados are praised as an amazing form of healthy fat. In this case, the bad rep just didn't make sense to me and I chose not to believe it.

Every day we hear some new nutritional theory contradicting everything we learned before. Learn everything you can, but remember you're learning theory, not necessarily fact. The only way you'll know what's true about the right food for your body is by keeping that detective cap on your own smart, introspective head.

Assignment: Be a Food Critic

Pretend you are a food critic this week and write up a description of the meal you are eating and determine how many stars to give it. Take a picture. Keep track: Are there any more foods that you want to move from "every day" to "once in a while?" Notice how you feel and start connecting more dots.

"THE FOOD YOU EAT IS ONE OF THE BEST HEALTH INVESTMENTS YOU CAN MAKE."

-LISA LEWTAN

CHAPTER XVII

PRACTICING THE P.A.U.S.E

"If knowledge is power, then curiosity is the muscle."

- Danielle LaPorte, author of *The Desire Map* and *The Fire Starter Sessions*

By now, I am hoping that you have learned how to analyze your own eating patterns without judgment and understand that there are so many reasons why we eat besides hunger. By putting on your detective cap, you have discovered which foods that you eat are affecting your moods, your thoughts, your energy, and your overall health on a daily basis.

Since I started using the Investigative Approach to understand my own hunger, habits, and triggers, I have become very careful to take a pause before eating and ask myself some key questions to determine if I am making good choices.

What am I really hungry for?

How will this food make me feel physically?

Can I stop after one bite?

Will I be disappointed in myself if I eat this?

Is this the best fuel I can be giving myself right now?

For example, I may ask myself, "*If you take one bite, will you continue to eat the entire chocolate bar until it is all gone?*" or, "*Are you only eating that bagel because you are feeling sorry for yourself?*" or, "*Will this cheese sauce make me feel sick?*"

I ask without judgment. I ask to create a conscious awareness about what I'm doing. I ask so that I can listen to my body and hear what she wants.

Sometimes I decide that I do not want to proceed with eating that food, *but many times I decide to proceed anyway and I do so with NO REGRETS!* I have no regrets because I made the choice and took time to think through the cycle of consequences and then, like the adult that I am, I accepted responsibility for the outcome. And this is how I started making better choices, stopped beating myself up, and became less food obsessed.

 The Pause

P - Particular: What particular thing am I REALLY hungry for?

A - Awareness: How will this food make me feel physically?

U - Urges: Can I stop after only one bite if my urges kick in?

S - Sadness: Will I be sad and disappointed in myself if I eat this?

E - Energy: Is this truly "premium fuel" that will energize me?

Let's look a little deeper at each part of the PAUSE:

The **"P"** in the pause stands for really tuning in to find the **Particular** thing I'm hungry for. If it's salmon I'm craving, or broccoli or a carrot, I may be craving something nutritious that my body needs. If it's a doughnut or a glass of wine or the bread basket on the restaurant table, however, it may be masking something else I am hungry for like a nap or a hug or some quiet time in nature.

The **"A"** in the pause is to remind me to use my **Awareness** to really think about the impact that eating a particular food has on my body. How will I feel physically after I eat it? Will it make me feel gassy and bloated? Will it make me feel sluggish? Will it make me feel light and energized? I want to take this into account and make a conscious and aware choice before I take the first bite.

The **"U"** in the pause allows me consider my **Urges**. If what I'm about to eat is a food that's a chemical trigger for me, will my urges take over? If I take one bite, will I eat the entire bag of Hershey's kisses? I know there are some foods that are big troublemakers for me.

Actually, there are many foods I have trouble with! Once I start eating them, I can't stop. Taking the pause gives me the opportunity to choose whether to proceed or not, accepting full responsibility of the outcome without judgment.

The **"S"** in the pause is to remind me of the emotional state that can surface after I'm done eating this particular food. Am I going to be **Sad** and disappointed in myself if I eat this food? Am I going to beat myself up one more time for not staying on track? If the answer is, "Yes," then I just pass. I am not interested in torturing myself any longer and am never again going to let whether or not I eat a cookie ruin another one of my precious days.

The **"E"** in the pause is my chance to remember that eating food is about the **Energy** it gives me. When I take the pause, I have a chance to ask myself if this food I'm about to eat is premium fuel. When I think of myself as a Ferrari it's easy to know that and I would never give a Ferrari sub-par fuel. Would you? Eating crap makes me feel like crap so I try to avoid it as much as possible.

Assignment: Take the P.A.U.S.E with You

Write down the P.A.U.S.E questions on a card and carry them with you. When you are about to eat something, stop to take the "Pause" and understand what it is that is really going on. It will help you realize that you always have a choice.

CHAPTER XVIII

FIGHTING OFF FOOD PERFECTIONISM

"Stop looking for the perfect diet, the perfect way to eat. Be willing to let your relationship with food be messy and uncertain. Perfectionism around body or diet or weight or eating is soul crushing and destined to create internal suffering and outward failure."

- Marc David, Founder of the Institute for the Psychology of Eating

As you continue to upgrade your food quality, slow down and understand the reasons why you are thinking about food all the time. I want you to be careful of a situation that I see all the time.

I notice that so many of the women I work with are living and eating in "black or white" land. Either "on a program" where they eat super clean and feel great or "off" the program where they fall back into the sugar/wine/bread downward spiral.

The worst part of the "off" cycle is that they beat themselves up and feel like failures. By the time they get to my office, they are frustrated, exhausted, and skeptical. Easy to understand why! My hope for them and you is that you strive to live in the land of eating "grey" rather than "black and white."

When it comes to eating healthy, it's not about perfection. It's about loving yourself enough to know that you deserve to feel great. It's about developing your own flexible eating plan and not sweating the small stuff when you get off track now and then. It's about doing the best you can on most days.

We all get off track, but some of us have simply learned how to get back on track a little faster and a little more often. I think that many people who are living in "food black and white land" are trying too hard to be perfect and, as a result, have trouble staying on that path for very long.

The Problem with Food Perfectionism
The problem with an "all or nothing" approach to eating is that it is unsustainable for long periods of time and by aiming for it, you may be setting yourself up for failure.

Sure it is great to set the bar as high as possible. It is this passion that helps us achieve and excel in life. It is also incredibly important to be at a healthy weight and to be happy enough to maintain it.

By focusing on the minutia of eating every minute of the day, not only are we putting ourselves into stress mode, but we are also not focusing on what is really important to us in our lives.

> "WHEN IT COMES TO EATING HEALTHY, IT'S NOT ABOUT PERFECTION. IT'S ABOUT LOVING YOURSELF ENOUGH TO KNOW THAT YOU DERSERVE TO FEEL GREAT."
>
> -LISA LEWTAN

What Motivated Me

Although I was really good at thinking about food and losing weight all the time, I have always been the world's worst dieter. Unlike all those people who can lose ten pounds by just shutting their mouths, it never worked for me.

My first diet attempt was in high school. I decided not to eat anything all day except for an apple. By that night, I was tired and depressed and I started crying. Sobbing, I said to myself, "I will NEVER do that again." And, for the most part, I never did. I never tried the cabbage diet. I never tried the South Beach diet. I never tried the Scarsdale diet. I did try some others later but I couldn't stick with any of them. I hated following someone else's plan.

I realized that the goal of "skinny" did not motivate me in any way. I just wanted to feel good inside and outside. I wanted to smile on a daily basis. I wanted to live a great life.

Don't Skip This Tip!
What is your true motivation
for eating healthy? Be honest!

Thinking We Have to Be Skinny To Be Happy

Thinking we have to be skinny to be happy reminds me that sometimes we are so focused on looking a certain way that we forget why it even matters. Somewhere along the way we were taught that if we are skinny we have no problems and life is perfect. If only we looked perfect then we would have the perfect partner, the perfect home, the perfect job, and the perfect children, even the perfect dog. Sounds pretty ridiculous when we stop and consciously think about it! Food perfectionism is part of our overall life perfectionism.

Don't Skip This Tip!
Are you a perfectionist in areas
of your life? How is it serving you?

I'm not saying it's not important to be at a healthy weight. It is important. I'm just asking you to explore what skinny vs. healthy means to you, especially if you worry about it and think about it all the time. What does it represent? Don't get me wrong. It's important to look good. I love looking good. **But I am keenly aware that it doesn't matter what I look like if I don't *feel* good.** And, even if I look great one day, it certainly does not mean my life is perfect.

What I know is that there are many super skinny women out there that are not enjoying life and there are many heavier women having a great time. It doesn't really matter if you're skinny or a little heavy as long as you are healthy and living YOUR amazing life. Being skinny is not the end goal. The end goal is being healthy so that we can live an amazing life and feel free and happy while we're fully alive.

Think about how much time and energy you are devoting to food perfectionism and repeat after me:

I WANT TO BE HEALTHY SO I CAN LIVE AN AMAZING LIFE.

Notice the difference - "*My goal is to be skinny so that I will look good*" vs. "*My goal is to be healthy so that I can enjoy my life.*" The key to happiness on this food grey scale is to find the right balance for you—a fully functioning body at a healthy weight and a life that satisfies YOU.

We may believe that all of our problems will disappear when we reach a certain random number on the scale, but will we be more loved? Funnier? Smarter? Probably not. So don't wait to reach a "*perfect*" weight to start living life fully.

Welcome Back Stress Mode

Another problem with food perfectionism is that every single time you disappoint yourself, which is probably often if you are living by rigid rules, punishing yourself with starvation, only eating super foods, or over-exercising, you are putting your body into stress mode which only works against you.

I get very sad when I hear stress inducing comments like:

> *"I was so bad yesterday."*
> *"I already messed up so I might as well keep messing up."*
> *"I don't eat carbs."*
> *"I won't eat it if it's not organic, locally grown, and non-GMO."*

I meet many clients who spent years counting daily calories or points or grams or ounces and have trouble giving up that supposed "discipline." Others incessantly compare themselves to other "perfect eaters" who they feel may eat less or cleaner than they do. And then others, who get so enthusiastic about healthy eating that they sometimes go a bit overboard and start feeling guilty if they eat something that is not what they deem healthy enough, as in the case above with the organically grown, locally grown, non-GMO. All of this is food perfectionism which provides the "I'm not good enough" feeling in another flavor.

My rule of thumb is to eat the best option available to you. Of course I would prefer to eat an organic, locally grown, non-GMO salad, but I can't always do that. If I am at a truck stop in the middle of nowhere, I will make the best choice possible and get on with it.

In order to have a good relationship with food, we must have a good relationship with ourselves. We need to start loving ourselves for who we are right now, complete with all of our bumps and lumps, and focus on building the best kickass life we can imagine. And, we must ditch our Inner-Critic Bitch (see the next chapter for more on that!)

Assignment: Find Your Fifty Shades of Food Grey
Do you find yourself alternating between eating so well and eating so *badly*? Take some time to think about this and start jotting down ways that you could begin to live in the land of eating "*grey*" rather than in "*black or white.*"

CHAPTER XIX

DITCHING YOUR INNER-CRITIC BITCH

"For some reason, we are truly convinced that if we criticize ourselves, the criticism will lead to change. If we are harsh, we believe we will end up being kind. If we shame ourselves, we believe we end up loving ourselves. It has never been true, not for a moment that shame leads to love. Only love leads to love."

**- Geneen Roth, author of *Women, Food and God:
An Unexpected Path to Almost Everything***

My Inner-Critic Bitch used to start her day by getting on the scale. If the number was within the three pound acceptability range, she smiled and reached for the tight fitting Lululemon top. If the number was even half a pound above the outer limit, panic set in, as did crankiness. She reached for the suck-it-in panties and nonstick clothing. The day was off to a bad start.

An Inner-Critic Bitch is a state of mind and, for the purposes of this book, is a voice in our head that spends way too much time worrying about the fluctuations on the scale and tummy flab and thus adding even more stress and cortisol to our already stress filled lives.

I don't remember exactly when but, somewhere along the way, I decided to ditch my Inner-Critic Bitch and switch.

Now, instead, I listen to my cooler Inner Healthy Babe who thinks I am "the shit!" On the outside I look pretty much the same but on this inside, since making the switch, I feel so much calmer and happier.

I named my Inner-Critic Bitch Frankie. Frankie used to obsess 24/7 about how to make me eat less. As a hungry girl with an extraordinarily healthy appetite, this was a big problem for me.

Together, Frankie and I tried counting calories, limiting me to "portion controlled" protein bars and shakes, and indulging only in high fiber cereal.

Unfortunately, I still walked around literally starving all the time. All I wanted was more food and I didn't understand why I wasn't full after three bowls of cereal, an apple, and a frozen yogurt.

Frankie begged me to control my voracious appetite and got very frustrated with me when I didn't comply, so I continually heard her voice in my head berating me and threatening me and obsessing about how I would keep my mouth shut, especially at restaurants and parties.

Screw that.

My Inner Healthy Babe, who I named Chelsea, reminds me to eat REAL food rather than fake, diet, non-fat foods, or foods that have been given squatter's rights on the supermarket shelves.

Thanks to Chelsea, I focus on nourishing my body with proper nutrients and eat without guilt or stress because the right foods really do fill me up. Not feeling starved all the time was one of the biggest reliefs of this decade for me. Not kidding.

Frankie used to worry that if I didn't get to the gym and burns at least 400 calories in spin class and then pump iron for at least another half hour, it didn't really count as a workout.

She also insisted that I do intense rock 'n roll heated power yoga (as opposed to the kind and gentle class) a few times a week because it wasn't in my best interest to spare ninety minutes if it didn't involve some form of pain—or so she thought.

Frankie was proud of me when I efficiently used the quiet time at the end of yoga class to think about the fifty things I needed to get done on my drive home but, ironically, after a few quick errands, Frankie had no problem with me sitting at my computer the rest of the day. She had checked off the workout box and that was all that mattered.

Nowadays, Chelsea tells me to move all day long. Whether it is walking, shopping, dancing, cleaning the house, walking the dog, or standing at my computer for hours while I work. Now, I find that I am rarely sitting down and Chelsea is thrilled.

> "RATHER THAN STARTING THE DAY BY GETTING ON THE SCALE, TRY STARTING WITH POSITIVE AFFIRMATIONS, A LITTLE GOAL SETTING, AND A FEW BULLET POINTS IN YOUR GRATITUDE JOURNAL."
>
> -LISA LEWTAN

Instead of meeting a friend for a salad with dressing on the side, I may meet her for a walk or a manicure. Rather than a night out for white tequila shots with the girls, we may try a dance class. Rather than starting my day by getting on the scale, I start my day with positive affirmations, a little goal setting, and a few bullet points in my gratitude journal.

Frankie used to push me to meditate because she thought it was something I should do. Not surprising that it just became another item on our endless to-do list.

Chelsea, on the other hand, didn't care whether I meditated or not as long as I managed to find quiet ways to relax, unwind, and BREATHE.

All that deep breathing made me calmer, more focused and more present in my relationships. Taking that time to be quiet and to breathe gave me the impetus to ditch some toxic, superficial relationships that were not serving me.

Chelsea reminds me that when I share a lovely meal with family and friends IT IS NOT ABOUT THE FOOD! It is about the love, the sharing, the connecting, the nurturing, and the experience.

Chelsea has also taught me that, even if some months I am carrying around a few extra pounds than Frankie would prefer I get rid of, none of my family members or real friends care one little bit.

Thankfully, Frankie packed her bags and moved out of my consciousness...to Hawaii. She pops in to visit every now and then but knows she is not welcome and keeps her visits brief.

Chelsea, on the other hand, can often be found dancing around the house in her Lululemons and is now my best friend and constant companion!

How to Ditch Your Bitch

Your Inner-Critic Bitch is the voice that you hear in your head that tells you that you are not good enough. Every time you hear a voice in your head say, "*I am such a loser because I ate that,*" or, "*I am not smart enough,*" or, "*I am not pretty enough,*" or, "*I am not thin enough,*" or, "*I am not competent enough,"* or, *"I am not worthy,"* that is her voice.

All of us have one, though in varying degrees. I have found that by naming your Inner-Critic Bitch you can become more aware of the negative thoughts popping up, have the power to separate them out as BS, and challenge their validity before they take up room in your psyche.

Start by choosing a name that you do not like but that you will remember. I chose Frankie. Now, go ahead and enter the name of your Inner-Critic Bitch right here:

The name of my Inner-Critic Bitch is:

_____

Okay, now that you've got the name, you've got the power!! To ditch your Inner-Critic Bitch, you need to pause when you hear her talk. Listen. Really listen.

Put on your detective cap. What are you hearing? Acknowledge the words. Challenge the thoughts. Are they true?

Now, pause, take a breath, and tell your Inner-Critic Bitch to take a hike!

Every time we believe that voice, she wins, and when she wins she gets more and more powerful. Just because she says it, does NOT make it true.

Your Inner-Critic Bitch probably didn't start out as a voice that wanted to control you. She probably thinks she's being helpful and encouraging but somewhere along the way her plan stopped working.

The good news is that just like changing a bad behavior habit, you can change the habit of how you think. The more you work on it, the more vigilant you become at identifying the voice, stopping the thought spirals, taking in that deep breath and challenging the truth. The more you work on it, the more you can reinforce this new way of thinking and being in your body.

Your Inner-Critic Bitch is all about appearances, about criticizing the surface details of what's on the outside as she projects it. She is the one who told you to stop wearing shorts (even though you love wearing shorts), that you haven't accomplished enough to go to the reunion, and that your arms are way too flabby to be seen in in a tank top!

Think back to all the times in your life when you beat yourself up internally because you didn't feel like you were SMART enough, or THIN enough, or SUCCESSFUL enough, or ATHLETIC enough, or INTERESTING enough, or just plain SPECIAL enough.

Shutting off this voice is necessary. It takes practice and time. It takes practice to change your thought patterns. Practice being your own cheerleader, your own advocate, and your own best friend. You've had enough time being your own critic. Retraining your brain to hear and empower your Healthy Babe allows for a kind of healing in the mind, body, and soul.

In order to truly ditch the bitch and switch, I also recommend incorporating some of the following actions:

Slow Down
As a Type A tech entrepreneur, I was trained in working fast and furious. Slowing down for a minute, a day, or a week was REALLY hard for me and I know it is for some of you too. In fact, I still find it challenging, but now I know how important it is for my mind and body to stay healthy.

I would love to say that you should meditate every day, and we will talk about that later in the book, but just start wherever you are. That may mean, for some of you, to just breathe. If you can do some deep breathing for a few minutes, go for it. If you can meditate, awesome. It's all good.

> # "JUST LIKE CHANGING A BAD BEHAVIOR HABIT, YOU CAN CHANGE THE HABIT OF HOW YOU THINK."
>
> -LISA LEWTAN

Be Kind
Treat yourself the way that you would treat your best friend or a baby. Be nice. Be gentle. Be loving. Be kind. Forgive yourself for not being perfect. Move self-care up a few notches on the priority pole.

Focus on ADD, ADD, ADD, ADD
Focus on bringing in better nutrition and more self-love. Focus with awareness on how the foods you eat help you feel rather than on how you look, and keep your eyes on the prize of real health while you keep adding more of what you love to your life.

Develop a Compassion Habit
Look. It's been decades since your Inner-Critic Bitch arrived on the scene. It will take some time to default to the compassion habit. Give yourself some time to really observe her and replace that voice with the one that's all about love and compassion.

Start by taking a look in the mirror today and try to really see yourself through loving and compassionate eyes. Rather than focusing on the bulging belly or the mushy tush or the fine lines around your eyes or aching stiffness in your lower back, STOP, and look at yourself the way others actually see you.

I have a feeling you might like that person you see a whole lot better than that person your Inner-Critic Bitch is always berating.

I have a feeling that it's this person that the people who love you see best. This person is gorgeous and fascinating and kind and successful and someone I would like to hang out with.

Lessons from My Grandmother
When I get stuck in the "I'm not good enough" mentality, I just think of my grandmother, who we all called Mama (pronounced Mumma). Mama was a really big part of my life growing up. She was one of those women that just oozed yummy, unconditional love.

She was soft and mushy and always looked really old to me from about as long as I could remember. She was usually dressed in a baggy housecoat type thing that I don't think they make anymore, but had her hair and nails done weekly at the beauty parlor.

Together we would bake cookies, go through old photos, and make Jell-O molds. Mama once said to me, "Lisa, nobody can take a Jell-O mold out of the pan as well as you can," and I beamed with pride. After that, I was always ready and willing to help.

Mama just had that way. She made me, and everyone else, feel so incredibly loved and special. When I look back, I chuckle thinking that, despite going to college at a time when few women did, Mama never learned how to drive a car, never got her ears pierced, and didn't really care about what she accomplished—and yet, she accomplished so much.

Unlike Mama, we women today are so focused on being perfect superwomen. We strive to get it all done, to be perfect mothers, to have perfect careers, to eat perfectly, and to have perfect bodies. It's exhausting just writing these words!

Mama wasn't caught up in any of that. She was just kind and loving and at the end of the day, she made you feel amazing.

So, whenever I get really caught up in this, "Ugh, I haven't done enough, I'm not good enough," and all that blah, blah, chatter I get in my head, I think of Mama and I remember, at the end of my days, if I have made people feel the way that Mama made me feel, I would consider my life a true success.

Be Prepared for Unexpected Visits
Unfortunately, even after you have kicked her to the curb, your Inner-Critic Bitch will sometimes come back to visit you when you least expect it.

Before you re-banish her, however, you should take a look at what she came back to say. Put your detective cap on and observe the interaction. If you're triggered, ask yourself why?

Once you figure it out, simply tell her you're doing just fine without her and send her on her way.

Challenge the thoughts and decide if they are truthful and useful and use the information to move forward without shame or judgment. Then, do some more investigation as to why she returned in the first place.

There are many different factors that can play a role in bringing your Inner-Critic Bitch back from vacation.

Here are a few:

> **Hormones** - The hormone fluctuations that take place during PMS, perimenopause, and menopause can really mess up our thought patterns. Notice if your thoughts change at various times in the month.

Eating Certain Foods - Notice if your thoughts change based on what you have eaten. Let's say I eat a piece of cake after promising myself that I wouldn't and I start berating myself. I hear my Inner-Critic Bitch enter the room and tell me things like, "You have no willpower. You suck. You will never lose weight if you keep eating like this."

Sleep - Notice if your thoughts change based on your sleep quality. When we are tired, not only do we crave comfort food, but our emotions can be affected as well. I always get sad when I am tired. That's when I start hearing, "Why haven't you finished that project yet? I thought you were better than that!"

So How Do I Banish Her Again?

These days, when Frankie comes back to visit, I see it as just a symptom. I put on my detective cap and, without judgment, say to myself, "Isn't this fascinating that Frankie brought those awful thoughts back. I really thought they were gone forever, but I guess not!"

I name it and I say out loud to myself, "Hey, Frankie, I hear you loud and clear. Thanks for coming. I've got this now."

Then, using the Investigative Approach, I look at what is going on in my life. I think about what I have been eating, my stress level, and my sleep patterns and start putting the pieces together.

Assignment: Dear Inner-Critic Bitch Letter

Write your Inner-Critic Bitch a breakup letter. Just like breaking up with anyone, sometimes you have to escalate the ways you say, "Get lost." It can be as simple as this:

Dear _____,

You suck. I no longer believe you, trust you, or value your opinion.

Have a great extended vacation in _____ and please don't come back.

Sincerely,   _____

CHAPTER XX

WATCHING YOUR LANGUAGE TO WATCH YOUR WEIGHT

"Happiness is when what you think, what you say, and what you do are in harmony."

- Mahatma Gandhi

In order to move away from food perfectionism, it helps to stop labeling food as "good" or "bad." I prefer to think about foods as "more often" and "less often." Yes, eating healthier is better for you, but putting a negative connotation on our food choices only fuels the fire of self-judgment and keeps us in that awful place of stress mode.

No Confession Required
Many of us have a need to confess our transgressions about food to others. Once we admit it, somehow we feel exonerated. We whisper, *"Oh my god I had three cookies,"* or, *"I wasn't supposed to, but I had a glass of wine."* For some reason we feel like when we state it out loud that maybe we'll be forgiven. Maybe we're not so bad.

When someone says to me, *"I was bad today,"* I ask, *"What did you eat?"* I might hear, *"Too much chocolate,"* or, *"Half the peanut butter jar,"* or, *"A brownie."*

Rather than berating them, I simply ask, *"Did you enjoy eating it?"* I am hoping they say, "YES," but more often I hear, "Not really. I'm really mad at myself for eating it."

If you ate for the love of what you ate, excellent! But if you beat yourself up afterwards, decide was it even worth it?

Instead of judging yourself, use the Investigative Approach and ask yourself, *why did I eat that entire bag of chips*? And learn your why. No need to beat ourselves up and no need to confess. Just put on your detective cap and say, "*Hmm...How do I feel? Not so good. Okay. Next time I'm going to think a little harder and maybe make a different choice.*"

And that's how we start getting real change.

The next step is to take a look at other things that we are saying that may need some reframing such as, "**I Don't Want to Deprive My Children.**"

Very often I hear sentences that make me want to cringe. "*I don't want my child to be deprived of Oreo Cookies*," is one of them.

When a parent wants to continue the Oreo tradition, they're simply setting up their child to struggle from the same sugar addiction that they are struggling with now. Whether or not it was part of your American childhood, your child deserves so much more than Oreos.

Your kids should not be deprived of love or attention. Your kids should not be deprived of a good education and enrichment activities. Your kids should not be deprived of the best nutrition available. As for Oreo's, save them for an occasional treat.

Food for Thought
Ask yourself, "Do I show my love through food?"
Then, keep asking, "When? Why? How? To whom?"

> "JUST BECAUSE A FOOD DOESN'T BOTHER YOU PHYSICALLY DOESN'T MEAN YOU SHOULD EAT IT. IF YOU ARE GOING TO BEAT YOURSELF UP AFTERWARDS, IT IS CERTAINLY NOT WORTH IT."
>
> -LISA LEWTAN

I Cheated on My Diet

Diets don't work and the reasons why diets don't work are that they were designed for someone else, not YOU. We are all different and each of us has a unique body type and health history. We all need to eat differently to feel good.

Most diets are based on deprivation and narrow food choices so it is natural to start craving foods that are "not allowed." This is then somehow deemed cheating. When you eat a healthy diet loaded with mostly nutritious foods, you don't feel deprived and you don't really think about the word or concept of cheating.

I can't stand it when people tell me they "cheated" on their diet. The word "cheat" means to act dishonestly or unfairly in order to gain an advantage. What advantage does eating junk food give you? If you really want it, just eat a bit of it, enjoy it and get back to healthy eating without the negative "cheater" self talk.

Eating healthy is not an exam, it's an honest gift to yourself.

www.HealthyHappyandHip.com

When you eat YOUR healthy diet, everything is experienced with an attitude of discovery and non-judgment. When you have a breakdown or get off track with your plan, instead of feeling bad, like you committed a crime, you just get curious.

My experience is this. When you start eating healthier you may find you just don't want the foods you'd "cheat" to get anymore. You start craving healthy foods. In fact, one of my clients texted me, "*I wanted to tell you I am starting to CRAVE vegetables! I even put spinach in my eggs which is a first and ordered cauliflower and broccoli as a side last night.*" She was way more surprised than me.

Reserve the Word "Deserve"
Do your find yourself saying, "I deserve a treat," and then rationalizing the brownie, the martini, or the candy bar?

After all, you worked a long, busy, stressful day. You managed to workout, pack the lunches, get the kids to school, sit in traffic, deal with your mother-in-law, negotiate the deal, file the claim, make the appointment, argue with the phone company about your bill, call the vet, order the gift, get to the market, write the proposal, pay the bill, hire the intern, fire the babysitter, help with the homework, make the dinner, have sex, prep for a business meeting, and collapse.

On those days, it's very likely that you'll say to yourself, "*I deserve a treat.*" What sounds better than a fresh baked tollhouse cookie and a glass of milk? Or a glass of wine?

Well, you do indeed deserve a treat, but that cookie is going to feel really great for a few minutes and then really awful for the rest of the night. And that glass of wine may easily turn into two or three glasses of wine that may turn into five or six bottles of wine each week. So what is the answer?

Maybe a treat is a few moments alone with a cup of hot tea. Maybe it is a massage. Maybe a treat is a warm bath, a stupid magazine, a call to someone special, a nap, reading or writing a chapter in your book, or five minutes of meditation. When we tap into what we really NEED, that treat is often something completely non-food related.

"I Don't Have Time" May Mean Something Else

Some things I hear all the time are, "*I don't have time for breakfast.*" "*I don't have time to exercise.*" "*I don't have time to meditate.*" Next time you hear those words come out of your mouth replace them with, "*It is not a priority.*" "It is not a priority for me to eat breakfast." "It is not a priority for me to exercise." "It is not a priority for me to meditate."

Think about the busiest people we know of—Beyoncé finds time to eat breakfast, President Obama finds time to exercise, and Oprah finds time to meditate. If something is important to you, I guarantee you will make time for it in your day so it might be a good time to start looking at your day and making some changes.

"I Will Start on Monday."
Making changes to your day-to-day diet doesn't need to start on Monday or after vacation or on the first of the month or after the party or right before the big date. Face it. Life is full of "eating events" all the time so it is never really the perfect time to start.

Many people take the "*I will start right after this special occasion*" mentality but the problem with that is that when you look at your life closely, every day can be a special occasion of some sort. Between birthdays, anniversaries, weddings, office outings, and every tradition's holidays, our daily schedules are jam-packed with reasons not to start.

Therefore, why not RIGHT NOW? As soon as you want to, ready or not, just start in the moment that presents itself. If you blew it at the eating event that happened earlier in the day, just start at the next meal or snack.

Food For Thought
What can I start doing right now to improve my health?

Change the Daily Phrases
Changing some simple daily phrases can help you change your mindset. Simply saying, "I don't want it," instead of, "I can't have it," is empowering. Here are some other suggested changes:

Instead of Saying:	Try Saying:
I will never eat this food.	I will not eat this food today.
I can't have it.	I don't want it.
I don't have time for breakfast.	I don't make time for breakfast.
I hate going to the gym.	I can move my body all day.
I messed up, so why bother?	I messed up, but I can recover.
I have no self-control.	I don't understand my triggers.

Assignment: Listen

Put on your detective cap and start listening to your own words and the words of those around you. Are you noticing any patterns? Are there some changes that you wish to make to your daily vocabulary? Start connecting the dots on how your words are affecting your weight and keep recording your insights!

CHAPTER XXI

WANNA IMPALE YOUR BATHROOM SCALE?

"If my weight were an accurate measure of my health, my beauty, or self-worth, scales might be valuable. But I broke up with that belief a long time ago."

- Isabel Foxen Duke, emotional eating expert

For many of us, the moment we see a number on the scale and start to think, "I need to lose weight fast," is the moment we start eating everything in sight. Our stress level goes up as does the anxiety and embarrassment that we're carrying around these five or ten or fifteen or more pounds. We wonder if everyone is looking at us thinking we are such a pig. We wonder how this happened so fast.

I used to get on the scale to punish myself. If I saw a really huge number I thought it would provide motivation for me to lose weight, but it actuality made me feel worse. I felt out of control, like a loser, and usually I'd be very depressed and anxious for the entire day.

On the other hand, when I saw a lower number, I would be so happy that I somehow rationalized I could eat more and would end up self-sabotaging my efforts by indulging all the more.

When I stopped weighing myself on a regular basis, I started just checking in with my body, counting my blessings, and feeling great. I didn't need a scale to tell me how I felt. I needed to be in my body to feel how I felt.

After a holiday, like Thanksgiving, or a vacation, I clearly look puffy and feel like stuffed turkey. Rather than stressing about it though, I just go back to my regular healthy eating and self-care practices and I know that by doing this, I will get right back to how I was shortly before the food fest. No punishment, no stress, no beating myself up.

And you know what? It feels a lot better.

> **Food for Thought**
> For some people, the bathroom scale is a useful tool. For other people, the scale is a weapon of mass destruction. Which camp do you fall into?

Is the Scale Your Friend?

If you weigh yourself once a day, a week, or a year just to check-in or if you find it a motivator to lose or maintain weight without feeling too bad about fluctuations, then go for it. The scale is your friend.

Is the Scale Your Enemy?

On the other hand, if you are letting a metal device determine your self-worth, you may want to reconsider. Can the number on the scale ruin your day? Are you weighing yourself multiple times throughout the day? Before the poop? After the poop? After the workout? Before bed? You are not alone. I hear this all the time. If the number on the scale has this type of negative power over you then you may want to skip it and just look in the mirror. The scale is not your friend.

Do You Dread the Weigh-In?

Do you stress out going to a checkup with your doctor simply because you know you will get weighed? Not sure why, but every year it totally stresses me out! I hate getting weighed at the appointment and start noticing that the thought of it starts creeping into my mind days in advance. As soon as I walk in the office, I start taking off my watch, my shoes, and as much other clothing as possible. I don't even know why I care, but I do. Do you? I've even refused to be weighed at some appointments simply because I didn't want to think about it that day.

> "STOP LOOKING FOR YOUR SELF-WORTH ON THE BATHROOM SCALE. YOU WILL BE REMEMBERED FOR HOW YOU MAKE PEOPLE FEEL, NOT HOW MUCH YOU WEIGHED."
>
> -LISA LEWTAN

You Are Not the Number on the Scale

I often hear clients say, "I want to weigh X." Even those at a healthy weight seem to always want to weigh five pounds less. When I ask them why, I usually hear things like, "I really like that number," or, "I think that is the number I should weigh," or, "I weighed that fifteen years ago and felt great." Sound familiar?

I work with all shapes and sizes and have found that what you weigh is no indicator of your happiness level. Getting to your desired weight may not make you happy but getting happy may help you get to your desired weight.

At the end of the day, people are going to remember you for how you made them feel, not how much you weighed.

Whatever peace you make with your scale, that peace is yours to keep. The scale provides just a single point of data and doesn't have to mean anything more than what you let it mean. If you feel like tossing it out the window, I will not stop you!

> "GETTING TO YOUR DESIRED WEIGHT MAY NOT MAKE YOU HAPPY BUT GETTING HAPPY MAY HELP YOU GET TO YOUR DESIRED WEIGHT."
>
> -LISA LEWTAN

Assignment: Create a New Way to Measure
Just for a week, don't get on the scale. Keep track of your smiles, your victories, and all the things for which you are grateful. See how that feels instead. Don't forget to keep track of how you're feeling and what you're grateful for.

CHAPTER XXII

ANATOMY OF A BREAKDOWN

"Imperfections are not inadequacies; they are reminders that we're all in this together."

- Brené Brown, author of *The Gifts of Imperfection*

Look. Even after you've figured out how certain foods affect you and you are on a good healthy eating track, you may not always be feeling calm, confident, and strong about your food choices. There will be times when you just have a breakdown. As Howie Day's song "Collide" says, "Even the best fall down sometimes," and it is especially true when it comes to healthy eating.

And that's okay.

What matters more than anything for your ongoing health and wellbeing is that when you fall down, you just get up, dust yourself off, and recommit to the healthy, happy way forward that you've designed.

Here is the story of one of my clients and the anatomy of her breakdown, along with the success strategies we put in place for her to prevent it from happening again.

Return of the Chocolate Chip Cookie Monsters
Sara was preparing to have people over to her house for a wine and cheese party. She thoughtfully chopped up some veggies and also prepared a fruit platter so that she would have healthy choices to eat rather than only the cheese platter. It was a plan of great intentions but, due to a few actions, it went terribly wrong and backfired.

Sara started picking at food while she was arranging her platters. Since she felt that the fruit was a healthy choice, she decided to munch on grapes.

She picked one at a time from the bowl so she had no idea how many grapes she was actually eating.

Sara poured herself a glass of wine to relax and then got ready for her guests.

> ## "SUCCESS IS NOT ABOUT PERFECTION. IT'S ABOUT HOW MANY TIMES YOU GET BACK ON TRACK AFTER FALLING OFF."
>
> -LISA LEWTAN

When her guests arrived, Sara felt like she had eaten too many grapes so she decided not to grab a plate. Instead, she just continued to pick, mostly at the fruit, for the next hour or so.

Sara used all of her so-called willpower to stay away from the cheese and crackers not realizing that she was giving her body a huge amount of sugar from the fruit and wine with no protein and fat to stave off her real hunger.

When her friend, Sophie, showed up with a plate of fresh baked cookies, Sara's sugar sensors were fired up, her willpower reserve was compromised from the wine, and her hunger was raging from the sugar spike.

The cookies smelled so good that she decided to have just one bite of a cookie, and then she ate one bite more, and then one more bite, and then a whole cookie disappeared.

{This is about the time the foreboding music starts playing because you know something BAD is about to happen!}

Sara found herself clinging like a barnacle to the counter that held the cookie tray while entertaining her friends. She grabbed a broken cookie because it didn't look good on the platter. Then she noticed the oddly stacked cookie next to it so she had to eat that one too to make the plate look better. Next came the cookie on the other side of the platter that was out of place. Sara's friends were picking at the cookies too, so she didn't feel so bad. It was fun. They kept going until all the cookies were gone.

We are very impacted by the eating patterns of those around us. When others indulge, we feel more comfortable doing so too.

Sara started beating herself up. She was upset at her lack of willpower and her indulgence. She also had a bellyache and noticed her mood shift. Needless to say, Sara felt awful.

To make matters worse, the cookies contained a lot of chocolate chips and the caffeine made her feel wide-awake.

After her guests left and she'd cleaned up, Sara took a sleeping pill to fall asleep since she had to get up early in the morning to be somewhere.

The next day, you guessed it, Sara was a mess. She had interrupted sleep and a body full of too much wine, the sleeping pill, and so much sugar. Sara had a huge dehydration headache and was in tears, feeling awful. Not only did she feel awful physically, but she was also angry with herself for once again falling prey to the chocolate chip cookie monsters.

Like many of us, Sara had the best of intentions and still ended up in a bad scenario. How could she have strategized to handle this situation better?

A Better Plan:
Step 1: Schedule a Small Healthy Meal Before Guests Arrive
Rather than picking at the grapes before her guests arrived, Sara could have scheduled time to sit down and have a small meal containing protein, healthy fats, and vegetables to make sure that her hunger needs were met without a sugar spike.

Step 2: Start Hydrated
Knowing that she planned on drinking wine, Sara could have started with a big glass of water or two to make sure that she would not get dehydrated through the evening.

Step 3: Practice the PAUSE
Before reaching for the cookies, Sara could have had a conversation with herself and, knowing that sugar was a huge trigger for her, honestly considered whether she could eat just one cookie, whether she would be upset if she ended up eating more, and whether she should just take a pass altogether.

Step 4: Make Conscious Choices
If Sara had decided to pass on the cookies, she could have eaten the fruit when others were eating the cookies so as not to feel deprived. Since she had already eaten a meal, the fruit would have been better as a dessert when she wasn't as hungry since she would have eaten less.

Step 5: Ditch the Guilt
If Sara did still decide to eat the cookies, she could have then proceeded without guilt. No self-flagellation, just investigation.

So much of this process is using the Investigative Approach and learning to view every experience we want to label as "good" or "bad," as a neutral learning opportunity.

By putting on her detective cap, observing what actually happened and looking back without judgment, Sara had the data to make better decisions going forward and to avoid feeling awful the day after her next party.

It's all about getting back on track, and then it's about getting back on track again.

See, it's human to have breakdowns. There will always be the occasional breakdown and you can observe, record, and learn from what you do in that breakdown situation to then strategize for the future.

Stay Cool When Your Train Derails

Sometimes, even after reading this book and doing this work with me, you'll end up off track again for longer than a night or a weekend.

Maybe you're going on vacation and you're using that vacation as a permission slip to eat however and whatever you want. Maybe you're giving yourself the summer or winter to do what you will with your body. Whatever you do, it's your life and your body. I'm not about to tell you what you should do with it. But I am ready to help you stay cool about it.

When you're ready to get back on track after a period of off-roading, just repeat the Eat to Thrive program and you will feel better within days.

Remember, winning this game is all about continuity and consistency. It's okay to mess up. We all do it. It's human. The key is just getting back on track again and again and again with no shame or judgment. And then, getting on track again.

Just keep getting up. Get up. Mess up. Get up. Get it right! Get up. Mess up. Get up. Get it right again! Just keep getting up and getting back on track.

Assignment: Be Prepared
Do you have an upcoming event that could prove tricky? Write out a plan in advance. Be sure to include a healthy meal and lots of water. Sometimes it makes sense to eat before you go so that you can concentrate on the people rather than the food!

SECTION V

CHAPTER XXIII

IS SPIRITUALITY THE NEW SPANX?

"The beauty of a woman is not in a facial mode but the true beauty in a woman is reflected in her soul"

- Audrey Hepburn

Growing up, I always thought spirituality was something found in an Indian ashram or in a new age crystal shop.

As a Jewish girl from Long Island, spirituality was simply not in my day-to-day vocabulary. I went to Hebrew school and to temple for holidays, but I counted the minutes until I could escape.

Religion, to me, was all about things you couldn't do or shouldn't eat. It didn't bother me that I wasn't a spiritual person. Truthfully, it wasn't something that I had ever even thought much about.

It was in a sociology class called Birth and Death at Brandeis University in the eighties where I was first introduced to the concept of mindfulness. We went around in a circle at the beginning of each class recounting an experience that made us feel truly alive.

This class, and the awareness exercise of the circle, was way more interesting than my discrete mathematics class and it truly made me start paying attention to those little miracles happening all around me.

Around the same time, I signed up for a meditation class on campus which I assumed was a tool designed solely to help me fall asleep in public places such the library or European train stations.

Sadly, as I entered the work world and motherhood, my short-lived practices of mindfulness and meditation vanished. Unknowingly, I started to spend my entire life in the past or in the future. I carried around my battle scars of the past with me at all times. For some reason (like many of you), I needed to remember every single hardship that had ever happened to me in meticulous detail.

I would replay the stories again and again in my head to make sure that no tidbit of pain was forgotten. "*This is what made me who I am*," I theorized. "*Who would I be without my war stories?*"

Often, I would get caught up in the thoughts that spiraled, "*Woe is me—I so deserve to comfort myself with anything and everything because I am suffering*," and I would fall into a downward spiral of sugar and despair.

At the same time, I was continually in a state of future planning. Planning my career, planning vacations, planning events, planning meals, planning everything. I took pride in my super active brain and planning abilities and had a good laugh on a trip to Thailand where my family surmised that I could never be a monk solely because I would not be allowed to plan!

I was rarely in the present. I don't know if it was too hard or if it was just a habit but, once again, it never occurred to me to even question it. For a smart girl, I was pretty dumb.

But then, all of a sudden, I got smart.

Okay, it wasn't actually all of sudden…it has been a journey of sorts but I had my own mini enlightenment.

By living in the past and the future, I was totally missing out on the PRESENT!

Although I had been told again and again that mindfulness was a good thing, no one really told me WHY it was such a good thing or HOW to live that way.

Mindfulness - So Here's the Scoop
I've come to understand mindfulness as a state of conscious awareness that allows me to focus on the here and now.

In a mindful moment, the past disappears and the future doesn't exist yet. When I am practicing mindfulness, I can tune in to my feelings and my body. I can hear the wise voice inside my head. I can also hear the birds chirp and appreciate a process rather than an end result.

I have a different ability to make choices when I'm making them from a place of mindfulness.

When we live in a mindful state, we are truly in the moment. At any given moment, even if our world is falling apart around us, we can access a sense of joy, peace and wellbeing.

> "WHEN WE LIVE IN THE PAST WE OFTEN GET SAD. WHEN WE LIVE IN THE FUTURE WE OFTEN GET ANXIOUS. WHEN WE LIVE IN THE NOW, WE CAN BE JUST RIGHT."
>
> -LISA LEWTAN

As I started practicing mindfulness and trying to be in the present, I stopped having to lug the suitcase full of pain around with me or plan any of my future interactions to avoid it.

I stopped harboring most grudges that may have once bothered me. I stopped dwelling. And as I started spending less time planning, I worried less and was able to check in with myself and provide self-care in a whole new way.

I would put on my detective cap and ask my body, *are you tired right now? Are you hungry right now? Are you feeling tension right now?* I did not judge, I just observed. I listened to my body and I gave it what it needed. I became free.

So What Does This Have to Do With Spanx?

I don't know about you, but when I wear Spanx I look and feel just a little bit better than without them. Even though I eat healthy and exercise consistently, there is something about that little extra constriction that makes me more confident. When I am more confident, I glow.

Well, mindfulness and meditation can do the same thing, but even more so. Mindfulness and meditation can make us glow from the inside out making us feel a whole lot better than before.

So much of the time we are running around, eating in the car, or relying on coffee to get us through the day. This pattern can put our bodies back into stress mode which, as we now know, is the same fear based mode we'd be in if a tiger was chasing us.

Food for Thought
What makes you glow?

Mindfulness and meditation can help us calm down, feel better, clear our minds, and radiate joy. Spanx can make us look better on the outside. Mindfulness and meditation make us look better from the inside out.

Start with Mindful Eating

Often, we eat in front of the TV or while we're in the car and have no awareness of the food we are eating. Is it any wonder we are not satisfied? By eating mindfully, we actually create a pleasurable experience and have a higher level of satisfaction.

Here are some strategies to help you stay in the conscious moment when moving food toward your mouth:

1. Start each meal with some deep breaths and a pause to become fully present to where you are and how you feel in your body.

2. Pay attention to the colors and smells of your food and think about how it made it to your plate.

3. Before taking the first bite, take a moment to think about how grateful you are to have this delicious food available to you.

4. Chew your food slowly, concentrating on taste and texture. Pay attention to the crunchiness, creaminess, and flavor of what you are eating.

5. Put your fork down between bites and take one to three deep breaths before picking it up again.

6. Eat your food sitting down at a table. Not in the car. Not in front of the TV. Not standing by the fridge.

7. Pause and periodically check in with your belly. *Am I full? Am I thirsty? Is this food satisfying me?*

8. Try to notice when you are about 80% full rather than 100% full and stop eating at that 80% point.

9. Trust from experience that with the food you have eaten so far you will be full shortly, and if you continue, you will move from satisfied to stuffed.

10. Before grabbing a snack to eat, ask yourself, *am I really hungry for food? Or am I hungry for something else? And is this the best quality of food available to me?*

11. If you are eating with others, really look at each person you're with and let them know that you see them. Try hard to be present and truly listen to what they are saying rather than just planning your response.

Food for Thought

We all want to be seen, heard, and respected. Mealtime is a great opportunity to really listen.

12. If you are eating alone, notice your thoughts and let them flow without judgment or unnecessary action. Just keep bringing them back to the eating experience.

13. Pay attention to the food you are eating and notice how it affects your mood and your energy. If you don't like the way you feel, do not berate yourself with negative self-talk, rather note the feeling and remind yourself before eating that particular food again in the future. If you feel good, note that too, and be grateful for that experience.

Move toward Mindful Living
So now you've tried some mindful eating exercises, and you've got some sense of what happens in your body and mind when you're in the present moment and making conscious choices.

It is often very difficult to learn to breathe and to live in THIS moment, but this is how we become calm in a busy, stressed, and food obsessed world.

How many times have you been so caught up in your thoughts that you arrive somewhere without knowing how you got there?

Personally, I had rushed through so many important phases in my life so that I could accomplish more that I missed out on so many precious moments. *Why did I need to be working while I was nursing my babies? Why did I need to be writing my grocery list while in yoga class? Why did I need to be on the phone during my nature walk?*

Mindful living is being where you are while you are actually there.

Throughout the day, ask yourself:

"Where am I?"

and answer:

"I am here."

www.HealthyHappyandHip.com

So What Is the Relationship between Meditation and Mindfulness?
Meditation teaches us HOW to be mindful. Meditation is NOT about relaxation. It is about being present without judgment. It's about learning to witness our thoughts, quickly releasing them, and getting back to the breath. It is about being right here, right now.

When we learn how to do this through meditation, we can bring the concept into how we live our daily lives.

In addition, meditation lowers stress and lets us get to know our true selves. Over time, a regular meditation practice creates new neural pathways and changes the brain in a protective way. The practice helps us even when we're not actively practicing because it gives us a new calm that lives as a sensory reality, accessible in all high stress situations, once we've created it in our mind and body. The bottom line is that meditation takes us out of stress mode, which is one of our continuous goals.

Regular meditation practice can make your healthcare bill a little lower, remove reasons for doctors to prescribe anti-anxiety medication, and lower your risk of depression. Meditation helps you sleep better. It teaches you how to let thoughts go so they don't keep you up at night.

Starting a Meditation Practice
I often hear, "*I am a bad meditator*," or, "*I could never sit still to do that*," but that is usually a sign that meditation is exactly what you need! Everyone's mind wanders, but the practice of simply returning to the breath is a great analogy for getting back on track again and again in life (as with food)!

When starting to meditate, it doesn't matter if you meditate for a minute or for an hour—just that you take the time to commit in whatever way you can to your new practice. And breathe.

We completely take for granted the importance of air. You can get a sense of how important it is to breathe when you think that a human being can live approximately four weeks without food and four days without water, but only four minutes without air. We are hungry for air! For my clients that are new to meditation, I recommend they start by simply sitting comfortably in a quiet place and breathing deeply in and out for one minute. Rather than thinking about their to-do lists, I have them just focus on the words "IN" and "OUT" as they breathe in and out. That's it. Try it right now.

Once you get the "sitting a breathing thing" down, the next step is meditation. Here are some tips to help you get a meditation practice going:

1) Guided Meditations are so helpful and I love to experiment with different ones all the time. My favorite is the Deepak Chopra/Oprah Series but there are new apps out all the time to help with this.

2) Consider Moving Meditations. Walking a labyrinth, Qigong, and Tai Chi are all forms of moving meditations that you may have heard about. However, walking and dancing may be more accessible to you in your daily life. Just being mindful, focusing on your breath and your body, rather than all the chatter in your head, can make any activity highly calming and clarifying.

3) Try a Meditation Class or Circle. Meditating in a group is a really cool and powerful experience. The shared intention of the group can be very impactful on the individual members.

4) Find an Accountability Buddy. As with any new habit, an accountability buddy can help you stay on track until the habit is set in place. Perhaps you text each other every morning or email each other every night. Just knowing someone is waiting to check in with you may very well keep you on track.

5) Pick the Right Time. Attaching this new habit to an existing habit makes it much easier to incorporate into our daily lives. I like to meditate right after my daughter leaves for school.

6) Find the Perfect Place. Weather permitting, I head outside and face the trees. Otherwise, it's off to my sunroom I go, where it is full of natural sunlight and quite peaceful. Having a designated location pre-decided takes one more potentially derailing decision out of the way.

7) Meditate with a Partner. When I finally convinced my husband to start meditating with me, my practice went to a whole new level.

Not only do we encourage each other to commit to the practice, but it also took our relationship to a place of deeper connection and intimacy. We start each session by looking into each other's eyes and end our sessions by discussing our experiences.

To the Naysayers

I know what you are thinking now.... *I can't do this. Meditation isn't for me.*

My mind is racing all the time. I could never keep still. Right? Nope.

Take it one moment at a time.

How Do Meditation and Mindfulness Affect Our Daily Thoughts?

Throughout your day, as the negative thoughts come in, you can ask yourself, is this a useful thought or not? And if it is one of those "not" thoughts, you can just observe the thought without judgment, take a breath and come back into the present moment just like you would with meditation. The same goes for food. If you get a feeling of hunger, ask yourself if it truly is hunger. If it is not, observe it and refocus on your breath.

Assignment: Take a Breath

Start sitting and breathing. If you can only do it for ten breaths, that's okay. If you can meditate, awesome. It's all good. Write down a few times in the day that would make sense for you to stop and breathe. Perhaps with your morning coffee? At a red light? Right after a workout? Before each meal?

Having a plan will help you make it a new habit.

CHAPTER XXIII

TRANSCENDENTAL TRICKS TO GET A QUICK FIX

"This is part of human nature, the desire to change consciousness."

- Michael Pollan, author of *In Defense of Food*

Tuning in to my body throughout the day has made a huge impact on my mindset. With even a few minutes of daily meditation and/ or stillness, I have learned to stay calm and grounded. It started as a "have-to-do" on my list, but it turned into a "want-to-do" within a few weeks of practicing. Now, it's how I recharge. When I meditate, I literally feel like I am an iPhone connecting to my charger. Sometimes I even feel the electricity run through my body.

In addition to meditation, I have some other feel-good tools that I keep in my tool belt:

Universe Reminders and Creative Visualization
Rather than using affirmations like many people do, I prefer to start my day with my reminders from the universe. These are statements that I repeat every single morning to remind me what is important in my life and how I can help serve others in the best way possible. Reminders are personal and pertinent. I change them up every so often.

Some examples include:
- I am grateful for my food, my family, my friends, and my good fortune.
- My body is healthy. My mind is brilliant. My soul is tranquil.
- Happiness is a choice and I choose it.
- Hard work, passion, and authenticity will help me achieve my goals.
- My purpose is to help others thrive and in doing so, I, too, shall thrive.

I always close with the question:
- What wonderful thing will happen today?

Then, I take a moment to actually visualize my day and EXPECT amazing things to happen. They often do and I am thrilled to find that they are sometimes exactly what I have imagined them to be.

Gratitude
Have you ever met a happy person that didn't radiate gratitude? So much of our attitude is based on what we focus our attention toward. By focusing on all the good we have in our lives rather than the misfortunes, we are attracting more good stuff to come our way.

Don't you always want to give more to the people who thank you for what you've given them? I know the universe works the same way.

Many people assume that focusing on gratitude is something to do when times are good, but it is when times are tough that a gratitude practice is truly necessary. It is easy to be grateful when things are going well, but during those times of breakups, deaths of loved ones, losing your job, loneliness... that's when the gifts of a daily gratitude practice can really be beneficial.

If you don't currently have a gratitude practice, here's an easy way to get started:

Take a blank notebook and, each day, just jot down five bullet points.

Don't overthink it. It may look as simple as this:

I am grateful for:
- Being alive
- Avocados
- It stopped raining
- My dog
- No joint pain
- My bed is warm and cozy
- I dropped my phone and it still works
- I got a great night of sleep
- My family loves me even when I am awful
- I love my life

> "BY FOCUSING ON ALL THE GOOD WE HAVE IN OUR LIVES RATHER THAN THE MISFORTUNES, WE ARE ATTRACTING MORE GOOD STUFF TO COME OUR WAY."
>
> —LISA LEWTAN

Try to write five bullet points each day. By the end of the week you will have 35 bullets. By the end of the year you will have 1,825 bullets. You will be spilling over with gratitude! What a beautiful keepsake of what you are grateful for in your life.

Spend Time in Nature
Even for us city girls, it is hard not to feel the transformative effects of watching the waves of the ocean, the pride of the mountains, and the lush expanse of a forest. In nature, beauty is everywhere. The air is different and the experience of being totally surrounded by something so mysterious and real can have lasting effects on our health, our psyche, and our relationships. To really feel grounded and alive, get outside as much as you can.

Food for Thought
For many, nature is religion. What is nature to you?

Connect with Your Life's Purpose
Viktor Frankl's *Man's Search for Meaning* had a profound effect on me. Frankl was a psychiatrist who wrote this book after his experiences in Auschwitz in Nazi Germany where he paid close attention to why some people had a strong will to survive and others didn't. In a nutshell, it came down to "life purpose." Without it, we are doomed.

On the day that I read the final page in that life altering book, I closed the book and, for the first time, asked myself, "What is my life's purpose?" I knew instantly that it was what I had been doing my whole life—helping people feel better about themselves and helping them to thrive. Once I became consciously aware of my life's purpose, all of my personal and professional goals fell easily into place.

Connecting to your life's purpose can give this busy, stressed, and food obsessed life much more clarity and focus.

Continuously Jump Out of Your Comfort Zone
Being a little uncomfortable now and then is not such a bad thing. It is really easy to always play it safe, but life can get a little boring that way. I highly recommend pushing the envelope every so often and doing things that you wouldn't normally do while still, obviously, using good judgment.

Last year my husband gave me an unusual birthday present that really tested me on this concept. It was a gift certificate for a photoshoot with a boudoir photographer.

Honestly, I was truly flattered but also deeply horrified by this gift. Posing in lingerie was not my ambition or fantasy. For years, I had actual nightmares that I had showed up naked at board meetings and school functions and, trust me, it wasn't sexy.

So, when my husband presented me with this unusual gift, I was quite hesitant. But why exactly? I wondered. Was I ashamed of my less-than-perfect-body? Was I worried about what people would think? That it would be tacky? That my kids would be mortified? That I dreaded lingerie shopping? Probably a bit of all of the above, but never one to ignore an opportunity to jump out of my comfort zone, I quietly whispered to myself, "You can do this."

The session turned out to be quite fun and the pictures, much to my surprise, came out tasteful and beautiful. Most importantly though, by doing the photo session and jumping out of my comfort zone, I felt empowered and alive.

Although I still haven't agreed to jump out of an airplane and go skydiving with my son, I do try to jump out of my comfort zone whenever possible!

Putting All These Tools to Use
The true test for the effectiveness of a toolbox is having to put the

tools to use. Unfortunately I had to test my tools in a big way recently and, much to my amazement, they performed way better than I could have ever imagined.

Last winter was a tough one for me and my family. Within a few months, my father-in-law died, our dog died, and then my dad died. A week later my husband broke his back in a skiing accident.

I had more than enough justification to fall apart, freak out, or consume an entire freezer full of cookie dough ice cream. In the past, I probably would have done just that. I would have let myself get caught up in the "woe is me—I so deserve to comfort myself with anything and everything" and I would have fallen into another downward spiral of sugar and despair.

But I didn't do that this time.

Instead, I slowed down, tuned in, and felt my feelings.

As the waves of grief and fear moved in and out of my body for those few months and for many months afterwards, I stopped and felt all of them and then let them pass. In between those moments of grief, there were still many moments and memories of pure joy and love and hope.

I couldn't always do this so well.

I was taught to be strong and strong meant not showing your pain. Strong meant holding it together. Somewhere along the road to strong-ness, I stopped feeling some of my feelings and buried them in comfort food or just about anything else that could distract me from the pain. Strong served me well until strong ended up eventually breaking me down.

Much to my own surprise, I was able to feel quite grateful. I was grateful that my father, father-in-law, and dog were all surrounded by love when they died. I felt grateful that my husband would heal and be fine, grateful for the worries that I didn't have, and unbelievably grateful that I could actually FEEL my feelings.

I'm also grateful for the road I've traveled away from all of that. I'm grateful for the ways I've learned to take care of myself even as life and death keep going on around me. I'm grateful for the calm and peace of health and happiness in my life.

Assignment: What is Your Life's Purpose?
Take a moment and ask yourself this question, "What is My Life's Purpose?"

Notice how things fall into place in all the areas of your life when you know and articulate your purpose. Prioritize your days to do the most important things first and pursue your dreams.

CHAPTER XXV

MOVE AND GROOVE WITH NOTHING TO PROVE

"Put on the music and dance now. Move those lower chakras, open your heart, and let your life force express itself like the most succulent, juicy fruit, the most redolent and colorful flower, or the loudest and most raucous song."

- Christiane Northrup, M.D., author of *Goddesses Never Age: The Secret Prescription for Radiance, Vitality, and Wellbeing*

Exercise is a crucial component of a healthy lifestyle. It has a huge impact on overall physical health, mental health, and weight maintenance. Sadly though, for many of us, it can often only make a small impact on weight loss.

First of all, when we exercise more, we are hungrier and want to eat more. Also, many people get in that "I worked out hard so I deserve a treat mentality" that can be so counterproductive!

Finding the right exercises that feel good for your body is just as important as finding the right foods to fuel you.

Again, if there's one thing I want you to get from this book it's the confidence to know that there is no one plan that works for everyone and only you can design the right plan for you. It took me years to figure this out but now I get to reap the benefits.

You Don't Have to Be an Athlete to Be Athletic

Exercise has had a huge impact on my life. Though I have worked out consistently since my twenties, it wasn't until my forties that I became a certified fitness instructor, an empowerment dance teacher, and (one of my biggest personal achievements) earned a black belt in Tae Kwon Do!

Growing up, however, unless you count high school field hockey (that I gave up to be on kick line), I was NOT an athlete. I might have been an athlete if I had grown up with different parents but mine did not think of sports as anything other than a distraction from academics.

There was that one time that my mom and I decided to take up running. Truthfully, I think we were seduced by the new Adidas bright blue nylon running sneakers that had just appeared on the scene. They were lightweight and unlike any other sneakers I had ever seen.

Together, with excitement, we laced up our new sneakers and headed out for our first run. I think we made it to the end of the block and mutually declared, "This is so not happening!" That was the end of our running career.

Fortunately, during college, aerobics arrived and I became a regular at the gym, moving from step class to spinning to weights and forever it went on. I started working out regularly simply in order to smile. I did it to have fun. If something didn't feel good anymore, I found something else.

The gym became a playground for me. The weights, bands, and bosu's all felt like toys and I loved the group energy.

Nowadays, rather than going to one gym, I mix up my workouts even more. My favorite studios are Physique 57, Btone, Soul Cycle, and so many more with amazing classes. I recently started using Classpass. com so that I can do different classes every single day of the week and never get bored. I'm also thinking about trying Crossfit.

Don't Miss This Tip
Be sure to mix up your workouts.
It's a great way to prevent both injury and boredom.

Unfortunately, my Inner-Critic Bitch used to make me feel bad about the fact that I was an "exerciser" rather than an "athlete" like so many of my friends. In fact, I remember coming back from an amazing bike trip with some of them and feeling quite distraught. Although I had a great time on the trip, it felt so competitive and intense that it left me feeling like an athletic loser.

When I got home, I actually called a sports psychologist to better understand what was making me feel so bad about myself on this trip! He said, "Hang out with people at the gym and see if you feel like a loser there." Nope. Not a loser. Problem solved in an instant!

So, even though I am probably not going to be running marathons or signing up for triathlons, I will always keep moving and grooving my body in as many ways as possible. And, I will keep smiling and dancing. No, I am not a particularly graceful dancer. In fact, as you will read below, I was a ballet school dropout!

Ballet School Dropout

In my formative years, I was always a trendsetter. I was rocking Danskins and tutus way before the eighties. With a Ring Ding in one hand and a Barbie in the other, I would dance my way through each room of the house. It was obvious, to me at least, that I was meant to be a dancer. But sadly, by age four, I was a ballet school dropout.

Over the years I went on to become a jazz dance dropout, ballroom dance dropout, hip-hop dropout and, most recently, a Zumba dropout. This may not seem like a big deal to you but for me it was a HUGE problem. You see, I have always loved to dance. I'm just not a "dancer."

Truth be told, I have this itty-bitty problem, which has put a damper on my dance pursuits. I cannot follow choreographed moves. I don't know exactly why, but it must be the same reason that I can't follow recipes or driving directions and, unfortunately, Google maps for dance is still in development.

Oddly enough, over the years, this has not deterred me from trying to find the right dance class for ME.

I searched and dreamed of a class with ZERO choreography. I wanted a place in the dance world for my "kind" because I knew deep down that I was not alone on this uncoordinated journey. I knew there had to be a flock of birds with my kinds of feathers.

My search turned up empty.

Fortunately, besides being a dancer-wannabe, I had a great track record as a successful entrepreneur. Staring me in the face was an unmet need so I set out to fill it. First, a market test. I created a class at my gym called Dance Party. We turned off the lights and turned on the disco ball and I was in Heaven, dancing crazy in my Lululemons. It was AMAZING!

Problem was that nobody else thought so. I quickly learned that most people who go to classes want instruction. They want some choreography. Oops.

Undeterred, I marched on…

By chance, while de-stressing at one of my favorite places, the Kripalu Center for Yoga and Health, I walked into the noon class called Yoga Dance and quickly realized there was NO choreography and that people were having a blast.

I was so excited that I ended up signing up for teacher training and kept going back for more. Over the next six months, I learned so much in my various trainings at Kripalu but surprisingly little about dance moves. Instead, I learned how to take off my armor, show my vulnerabilities, share my wisdom, and slay my dragons all at the same time.

What I finally learned was that dance is not about following someone else's moves but rather it is emotional expression in its purest form. It is laughter. It is tears. It is romance, despair, elation, and frustration all at the same time disguised as shimmies and shakes.

No wonder I couldn't follow someone else's steps.

I went home and created my own class where I had been able to not only find my own moves, but to help others feel empowered and sexy and happy.

Together, we breathed and stretched and danced our hearts out and made lots of noise and then peacefully relaxed. The best part was that there was NO CHOREOGRAPHY, just suggestions. We laughed and cried and sweat. It was magical and it was what I had been searching for my whole life. So, in the end, I did become a "dancer", but more importantly, I became ME.

Crazy Thought: Ditch the Data
One of the things that I love about dancing is that, while I am doing it, I am having fun and am not thinking about calories burned or distance travelled. Call me crazy, but when it comes to working out, I hate data. It takes me out of how I feel and into some numerical analysis that doesn't really mean anything to me. In fact, it puts me right back into stress mode.

Once I stopped thinking about calories burned, heart rate, vo2max, metabolism, RPM's and the number on the scale, I appreciated my body in a whole new way. Now I just try to move my body in many different ways each week and have a really good time while I'm doing it. This helps me avoid injury and get the most out of the time I give myself at the gym.

> "DANCE IS NOT ABOUT FOLLOWING SOMEONE ELSE'S MOVES. IT IS EMOTIONAL EXPRESSION IN ITS PUREST FORM."
>
> -LISA LEWTAN

You're Not Lazy, Just Tired.

Often times, when I work with a client who is not motivated to exercise, we put on our detective caps and try to figure out why. "I know it's good for me, but I just never feel like doing it," is something I often hear. We use the Investigative Approach and often find out that the reason she doesn't want to exercise is because she is exhausted!

I don't know about you but when I am tired, my workouts are hugely impacted. In fact, after a bad night's sleep, I may choose to take a long walk rather than hitting the gym or taking a class. If I was a person who didn't like to workout to begin with, there is no way that I would even be motivated to take that walk on an exhausted morning. Is that lazy or is that tired? You decide.

Getting good sleep is critical if you want to develop a regular exercise routine. If you are a person who just thinks of yourself as lazy, I ask you to put on your detective cap and question that belief. Just consider the fact that you may just be really tired.

> "TAKE A DATA VACATION. FOR THE NEXT WEEK STOP THINKING ABOUT CALORIES BURNED, HEART RATE, VO2MAX, METABOLISM, RPM'S, AND THE NUMBER ON THE SCALE. THIS IS HOW EVERY OTHER ANIMAL ON THE PLANET LIVES."
>
> -LISA LEWTAN

Assignment: Make Your Moves

How about trying moving more simply because it feels good? Movement is an ideal way to release a buildup of physical tension. You don't need to run ten miles or have pain to feel great. Move in ways that feel good for YOUR body.

Did you dance, bike, or hike as a kid? You may want to revisit these activities.

Unless you are in training mode for a competition, how would it feel for you, as an experiment, to take a break from the data for a day or a week or forever? Let me know!

CHAPTER XXVI

WHAT YOU DRINK COULD BE A MISSING LINK

"Nothing would be more tiresome than eating and drinking if God had not made them a pleasure as well as a necessity."

- Voltaire

Many times that we think we are hungry, we are actually just thirsty. Most people walk around in a state of semi-dehydration and are just not aware of it. In fact, by the time we actually feel thirsty, we are already somewhat dehydrated.

Others fill their days drinking too much of the wrong thing, like coffee loaded with extras, sodas (both diet and regular), sugary sports drinks, sugar loaded smoothies, and even some seemingly healthy juice drinks that are loaded with sugar.

Once again, it's time to don your detective cap and take a look at how your body responds to what you drink.

Think Before You Drink
There are aisles and aisles of beverage choices. Here's a list of some of my absolute favorites and some of the things I doubt I'll ever put to my lips again.

Water
Water is the best. Drink it hot. Drink it cold. Drink it at room temperature.

Add a lemon. Drink it anyway you like, as long as you drink a lot of it. Depending on how active you are and your size, you should aim to drink eight to ten glasses of water a day. Dehydration can lead to headaches, fatigue, muscle cramps and aches, and mistaken hunger.

Here are some tips to increase your water consumption:
- Starting your day with hot water and lemon is refreshing and detoxifying. Make it a habit to have a full cup before moving on to coffee.
- Buy a 64-ounce pitcher and fill it up in the morning. Each time you fill your glass or water bottle, fill it from the pitcher. By the end of the day, your pitcher must be empty and you will know that you drank at least eight glasses of water!
- Infusion pitchers are a great way to add flavor to your water without adding needless chemicals or sweeteners. My favorite combo is grapefruit and fresh mint.

Take note of how much better you are feeling while getting enough water. Dehydration causes so many symptoms that we often associate with other causes. When you connect a new habit with a good feeling, you have more likelihood of making it part of your life plan.

There are many apps out there to remind you to drink water. They beep hourly to remind you to take a drink. Another trick is to set an hourly alarm on your phone reminding you to drink.

Herbal Tea
Drinking herbal tea is a great way to get extra water into your body. It is naturally caffeine free and does not contain the extra chemicals found in "decaffeinated" tea. Drink it hot in the winter to warm you up and cold in the summer to cool you down!

Watch Your Body for Dehydration Clues!
If you pull up the skin on the back of your hand and let go, it should bounce back to its original position quickly. If not, you may be dehydrated. There are also other clues that our bodies will give us when we start to pay attention.

My client, Leslie, was on a long bike ride with a group while vacationing in Arizona at an amazing spa called Canyon Ranch. It was a hot day and they went out early in the morning to avoid the heat. Leslie, afraid that she would not have access to a bathroom if needed on the trip, didn't drink much that morning in advance of the ride.

Somewhere along the ride, Leslie noticed that she was riding with her eyes closed and thought in her blurry mind that it might be a good idea to take a break. She vaguely remembered pulling over, telling the group leader what was happening, hearing screaming about code something or other, and being forced to drink fluids and rest.

The highly-trained and caring staff took her back to the lodge where she instantly became aware of her nausea and a big green vein protruding in the middle of her face. Her husband labeled it the "dehydration indicator vein." From that point on, when Leslie looks in the mirror and sees the green vein showing, she knows that she needs water fast!

Soda

I have to admit, I am downright shocked when I see people still drinking soda. There is nothing of any nutritional value entering your body when you drink soda. You have heard it all before so I won't go into it, but this is one of my only NEVER foods. Even diet soda. Give it up!

Food for Thought

If you are still drinking soda, now might be a good opportunity to ask yourself, "Why?"

Alcohol

More and more of my female clients are concerned about their alcohol habits. If you are drinking alcohol every day, you may want to explore why this is happening. Are you using it as a stress reliever? Do you prefer to drink rather than eat? Does it help you relax socially?

Food for Thought
Lately, I have been seeing many clients that crave wine every evening before dinner. At first, they think it is about the wine but, for many, they are actually hungry and have gotten in the habit of drinking wine before eating food. When they start eating food instead of drinking wine at that time, the craving tends to disappear.

Not only are teenagers faced with peer pressure about drinking, adults are often described as boring, straight-laced, or simply not fun if they decide to take a pass. If you feel weird NOT drinking at a party or a dinner with friends, keep these ideas in mind:

- If your underage child was at a party and was given a drink, what would you HOPE that he/she would say? Hopefully your answer is, NO. If you would expect your child to be able to say it, why can't you say no to a drink? No judgment, just notice.
- Fill a wine or martini glass with sparkling water and a lemon and no one will ever suspect anything.
- Then there's the truths you can try: "I'm on antibiotics and can't drink!" Or, "I don't drink during the week." Or, "I have a big day tomorrow."

Ultimately, you're the only one in charge of what you consume and you're the only one who will feel and endure the after effects of all you drink. It's good to feel good—and you deserve to feel good in a very different way than you deserve a drink. Keep in mind that every glass of wine is like eating a small dessert. Would you eat three desserts with dinner every night?

Juice

Believe it or not, a glass of orange juice can have as much sugar in it as a soda. You are much better off eating the orange, which has the added benefit of fiber. Even some seemingly healthy green juices, depending on their ingredient list, can contain very high levels of sugar as well. Unless you are making your own (with mostly vegetables I hope), then please be sure to read nutrition labels carefully.

Caffeine

After hearing at age nineteen that caffeine would make me age, I gave it up completely for the next twenty-seven years. Yes, I made it through all my years starting the technology company (complete with all-nighters) and through raising three babies without coffee!

Over those years, I read everything that I came across regarding caffeine trying to show my coffee enthusiastic husband how smart I was to abstain. Over and over again, I found information saying that a cup of coffee or two was good for me and could possibly help prevent diabetes, stroke and dementia.

After years of serious thought, I brought back a cup of coffee into my morning and never looked back. I love the taste, the ritual, and how it helps me feel stronger in my workouts and clearer in my thoughts.

Too much coffee, however, can put a tremendous strain on your adrenal glands and other bodily functions. In simplest terms, when you drink too much caffeine, you stop hearing your body talking to you.

Our bodies tell us when we are tired so that we can get rest, not so we can keep drinking more coffee. Having an extra cup once in a while is no big deal but if you are drinking coffee all day long, it is time to take look at your lifestyle and make some changes.

Lately I have been experimenting with adding grass-fed butter and coconut oil to my morning coffee. Note the word "experimenting." What this means to me is, *"HOW DOES MY BODY LIKE THIS?"* In truth, some days I find it quite filling and other days not so much.

Again, it is all trial and error.

Assignment: Drink Up!
Challenge yourself to drink 64-ounces of water every day this week. Note how much better you feel!

"OUR BODIES TELL US WHEN WE ARE TIRED SO THAT WE CAN GET REST, NOT SO WE CAN KEEP DRINKING MORE AND MORE COFFEE."

-LISA LEWTAN

CHAPTER XXVII

IF YOU DON'T SLEEP, YOU MAY WEEP

"There is a time for many words, and there is also a time for sleep."

- Homer, author of *The Odyssey*

I would be shocked if you, at this point, are one of those people who poo poo the importance of sleep. Not only can lack of sleep result in lack of memory, irritability, impatience, inability to concentrate, and moodiness, but too little sleep can leave you tired and unwilling to do the things you like, including having sex and exercise. Too little sleep impairs immune function, alters our hormones levels, keeps us in stress mode, and can make us food obsessed!

Personally, when I don't sleep, I weep. In fact, when I am sad, the first thing I do is put on my detective cap and think about why I am so sad. More often than not, the answer is, "*I AM TIRED.*"

Going to bed too late, waking up too early, waking up in the middle of the night to go to the bathroom, or dealing with a busy, stressed, obsessed brain that prevents us from falling asleep (much less staying asleep), has left many of us EXHAUSTED. Throw in some young children, work pressure, pets, and jet lag and we are often waking up exhausted, stressed, harried, and late.

We all know plenty of people who claim they don't need much sleep, and for some people that may be true. But for many of those five hour a night sleepers, they get caught in the I-need-six-cups-of-coffee-each-day habit. Because they automatically reach for coffee when they feel sluggish, they never really hear what their bodies are trying to

> ## "TOO LITTLE SLEEP CAN IMPAIR OUR IMMUNE FUNCTION, ALTER OUR HORMONE LEVELS, AND MAKE US FOOD OBSESSED!"
>
> -LISA LEWTAN

tell them in terms of health. They never hear their body say, "I NEED A NAP!"

My client, Kelly, worked long hours in a highly demanding job. After coming home and eating a quick dinner, she was back at her computer until late at night. Often she would get to bed at midnight but every so often it was as late as 2am before her head hit the pillow. She was tired, unhappy with her weight, and slightly depressed. Though she came to me in hopes of losing some weight before a big speaking engagement, through the Investigative Approach, we quickly realized that no matter how much kale she ate, it wouldn't make a difference until she started getting more sleep.

Kelly made a concerted effort to get to bed earlier. It was hard at first for her to create personal boundaries from her work, but she quickly realized that with a regular pattern of better sleep, she was more productive at work and didn't need to work as many hours. With the extra time created from working less, Kelly found more time to get to the gym, shop for fresh food, and was able to finally accomplish her goals.

In order to give yourself the best chance for a restful night's sleep, you need to start winding down hours before bedtime.

Here are some tips to help you get a better night's sleep:
- Write down a to-do list for tomorrow to clear your head.
- Consider a relaxation tape or evening meditation.
- Jot down some victories you experienced during the day and thoughts of gratitude.
- Turn off technology two hours before bedtime.
- Finish eating and drinking alcohol a few hours before bed.
- Start dimming lights to let your body know night is coming.
- Remove technology from the bedroom. Your bedroom should only be used for reading, sleep, and sex.
- Darken your bedroom by covering windows and clocks.
- Keep your bedroom cool.
- Just like you have rituals for putting your kids to bed, consider coming up with a list of your own like taking a warm bath, reading a chapter in a calming book, and smothering your feet in lotion.
- If you wake up in the middle of the night, don't panic. Use your deep breathing and just try to rest.

Assignment: Get Some Sleep!
Prioritize sleep by scheduling it in your calendar. Make it as important to you as the big meeting you spent all your sleep time preparing for. See if you can notice the improvement in your health, your relationships, your work performance and your wellbeing when you move sleep up the priority pole.

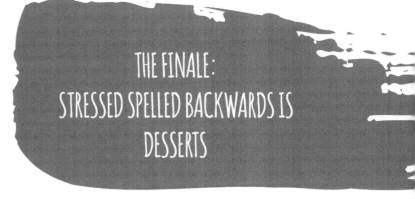

THE FINALE:
STRESSED SPELLED BACKWARDS IS
DESSERTS

SECTION VI

CHAPTER XXVIII

FINDING CALM

"What we think, we become."

- Buddha

I thought long and hard about what I wanted you to walk away with after reading this book. There are so many books out there, many of which are piled up on my night table right now, that offer a lot of theory and maybe a diet plan.

One of my clients described these types of books best. "You follow it for as long as you follow it and then you fail at it, and then it ends up in the garage sale or the giveaway pile at the charity pick up."

Though I love having a library full of those books, I didn't want to write one of those books.

The book I wanted to write, and the book I hope you just read, is one that helps you move forward with a sense of calm and a feeling of empowerment. A book filled with gentle wisdom and helpful strategies designed specifically for busy, stressed, and food obsessed superwomen like us.

Going forward, try to remember the following:
- Put on your detective cap and use the Investigative Approach to figure out the right choices for your unique body and life.
- Challenge your thoughts. Just because you think it, does not make it real. Thinking about food all day does NOT mean that you are actually hungry all day.

- Take a look at your life and see if you are spending time doing the things you love, are hanging out with the people who appreciate you, and are filling your body with premium fuel.
- Understand how certain foods affect your moods and your unique chemical composition.
- Rather than beat yourself up for eating something you didn't want to eat, simply put on your detective cap and say, "Hmmm, that's interesting that I ate that when I didn't want to." You can then figure out your why and start making strategies for the next time.
- Figure out what you love to do and what you long for and bring those things into your life.
- Question why you are so busy and stressed and see if it is required or desired.
- Practice the P.A.U.S.E. and give yourself a chance to take a breath, make a good choice, and respond instead of react.
- Remember that success is not perfection, it's about consistency most of the time.
- Keep in mind that when you get off track, you can simply get back on track again. And again. And again.
- Don't forget the importance of breath and have a toolkit filled with personal spirituality tools to bring you tranquility and peace.
- Recognize that thinking about food all the time is a symptom, not the cause. Use it as an opportunity for exploration and growth.

Keep in mind that our bodies and the world we live in are constantly changing. Just because we can figure out what works right here and now for our bodies doesn't mean it will always work. Just put on your detective cap and approach your body's changes with a simple attitude of inquiry instead of anxiety.

We deserve to feel great. Taking care of ourselves is about giving ourselves the best that we can so that we always feel amazing. Why NOT??

Look in the mirror and tell yourself that you are important, beautiful, smart, deserving, creative, compassionate, inspiring, kind, caring, and good enough just the way you are. And remember:

I Believe in YOU!

Looking For Community?

Lisa Lewtan is a Healthy Living Strategist and the founder of Healthy, Happy, and Hip. Lisa helps superwomen slow down, chill out, develop a better relationship with food, look good and feel great. Lisa offers private coaching, workshops, online courses, and women's retreats.

To Stay in Touch and Learn More with Lisa Lewtan, Visit:
Website: HealthyHappyandHip.com
Facebook: Facebook.com/HealthyHappyAndHip
Twitter: Twitter.com/LewLew2
Instagram: Instagram.com/ HealthyHappyAndHip
Pinterest: Pinterest.com/lewlew2

Be sure to join the site as a subscriber so that you can learn about launches and offers, workshops and retreats, as well as the schedule for upcoming in-person and online programs.

Work with Lisa One-On-One
Lisa accepts a limited number of one-on-one clients each year. To learn more about this, email Lisa@HealthyHappyandHip.com

Book Lisa as Your Keynote Speaker
Need a speaker at your next conference, workshop, retreat, or gathering? Lisa presents educational, team-building, and fun presentations. Signature talks include:

- Busy, Stressed, & Food Obsessed
- How to Ditch Your Inner-Critic Bitch
- To Look Great, Spirituality May Work as Well as Spanx
- One Girl's Cupcake is Another Girl's Crack Cocaine

Email: Lisa@HealthyHappyandHip.com for more information or just to say hello!

Invite Lisa to Your Book Club
On www.HealthyHappyandHip.com, you can purchase the "Book Club Package" which includes fifteen copies of this book along with a link to schedule Lisa for a guest appearance at your book club meeting via Skype!

A Note Of Thanks

I could never have imagined this book writing journey without the support of so many amazing people. I am deeply grateful to all of you who took the time to ask me, "How's the book going?" Those little words kept me going day after day!

Thank you to all the men and women in my Healthy, Happy, and Hip orbit that have shared their struggles and victories with me. Whether you are a one-on-one client, have participated in one of my group programs or retreats, come to my monthly support group, participated in my Facebook group, or commented on one of my articles or posts, your enthusiastic feedback, insights, and smiles continually brighten my day.

Thank you to Abby Rodman, Barbara Wasserman, and Pam Wilsey for your encouragement, brainstorming, and camaraderie and to Nancy Hill, Claudia Schappert, Betsy Rosen, Marci Cohen, Claudia Crain, Samantha Bartfield, Gena Barenholtz, Donna King, Andy Schiller, Rachel Haims, Nicole Buchman, Stephanie Dodson, Susan Solomont, and Bonnie Rosenberg who have been my ongoing cheerleaders in my Healthy, Happy, and Hip journey.

Thank you to Joshua Rosenthal and Lindsey Smith for giving me the tools and inspiration to truly think beyond the book and to Marilena Minucci, Abby Seixas, and Nina Manolson for your trusted wisdom and guidance. Thank you to Rochelle Lurie who was the first person ever to say to me that I should consider writing and to Ronna Benjamin and Felice Shapiro at BetterAfter50.com who published my first article ever, giving me the validation that people wanted to hear what I wanted to say.

Thank you to Beth Benson, my book doula, who made the journey so much more fun and whose endless cheer, encouragement, and eternal optimism will always be deeply appreciated and to Sam Smith, who's album, In the Lonely Hour, played over and over and over again while I wrote this book. I simply couldn't write without it playing in my ear.

Thank you to my parents who somehow installed the "don't quit" mantra into my head and to my children, Lexi, Tyler and Devin, for teaching me, loving me, inspiring me daily, giving me purpose in life, and for keeping me humble.

And lastly, but most importantly, a big thank you to my husband Stuart. You are my best friend, soul mate and partner in life. From the day I met you, you have pushed me to think bigger, push the boundaries, and go for my dreams. I could never have written this book without your support and encouragement. You are my hero.

{SNEAK PEEK FROM MY NEXT BOOK!}

Relationship Inflammation

"The recipe for any loving, healthy relationship - be it with yourself or others - is a simple one: Ask, listen, truly hear, repeat."

-Abby Rodman, author of Without This Ring

I have defined my own term "**Relationship Inflammation**" as a state in a relationship when the two parties are in a heated and painful state as the result of a disagreement or incident.

When people are fighting, they're inflamed. They're red. They're angry. Just like in our bodies where we must reduce inflammation in order for healing to begin, the same applies to relationships.

Even the calmest and coolest of us can be taken to a highly agitated state in the company of some of those closest to us. Working through some of these issues can be so gratifying, but has to be done in the right way.

To be continued...